KT-443-421

Keown/Martin/Petty/Scott, *Foundations of Finance: The Logic and Practice of Financial Management*, Fourth Edition

Keown/Martin/Petty/Scott, *ActiveBook, Foundations of Finance*, v. 2.0

Kim/Nofsinger, *Corporate Governance*

Mason/Merton/Perold/Tufano, *Cases in Financial Engineering*

Mastering Finance CD-ROM

Mathis, *Corporate Finance Live: A Web-based Math Tutorial*

May/May/Andrew, *Effective Writing: A Handbook for Finance People*

Nofsinger, *The Psychology of Investing*

Ogden/Jen/O'Connor, *Advanced Corporate Finance: Financing Policies and Strategies*

Rejda, *Social Insurance and Economic Security*, Sixth Edition

Rivera-Batiz/Rivera-Batiz, *International Finance and Open Economy Macroeconomics*, Second Edition

Scholes/Wolfson, *Taxes and Business Strategy: A Global Planning Approach*, Second Edition

Seiler, *Performing Financial Studies: A Methodological Cookbook*

Shapiro/Balbirer, *Modern Corporate Finance: A Multidisciplinary Approach to Value Creation*

Sharpe/Alexander/Bailey, *Investments*, Sixth Edition

Sinkey, *Commercial Bank Financial Management*, Sixth Edition

Taggart, *Quantitative Analysis for Investment Management*

Trivoli, *Personal Portfolio Management: Fundamentals & Strategies*

Van Horne, *Financial Management and Policy*, Twelfth Edition

Van Horne, *Financial Market Rates and Flows*, Sixth Edition

Van Horne/Wachowicz, *Fundamentals of Financial Management*, Eleventh Edition

Vaughn, *Financial Planning for the Entrepreneur*

Weston, *Cases in Dynamic Finance: Mergers and Restructuring*

Weston/Mitchell/Mulherin, *Takeovers, Restructuring, and Corporate Governance*, Fourth Edition

Winger/Frasca, *Investments*, Third Edition

Winger/Frasca, *Personal Finance: An Integrated Planning Approach*, Sixth Edition

For more information on finance titles from Prentice Hall, visit us at *www.prenhall.com/finance*

CORPORATE GOVERNANCE

KENNETH A. KIM

State University of New York at Buffalo

JOHN R. NOFSINGER

Washington State University

UPPER SADDLE RIVER, NEW JERSEY 07458

Library of Congress Cataloging-in-Publication Data

Kim, Kenneth A.
    Corporate governance / by Kenneth A. Kim, John R. Nofsinger.
    p. cm.
    Includes bibliographical references and index.
    ISBN 0-13-142387-8
      1. Corporate governance—United States. I. Nofsinger, John R. II. Title.

HD2741.K4713 2003
338.7'4—dc21

2003054184

Senior Acquisitions Editor: Jackie Aaron
Editor-in-Chief: P. J. Boardman
Editorial Assistant: Francesca Calogero
Executive Marketing Manager: Debbie Clare
Marketing Assistant: Amanda Fisher
Managing Editor (Production): John Roberts
Production Editor: Kelly Warsak
Production Assistant: Joe DeProspero
Permissions Supervisor: Suzanne Grappi
Manufacturing Buyer: Michelle Klein
Cover Design: Lisa Boylan
Cover Illustration: Thierry Cariou/CORBIS
Full-Service Project Management: Tempe Goodhue/nSight, Inc.
Composition: Laserwords
Printer/Binder: R.R. Donnelly & Sons Company
Cover Printer: Phoenix Color Corp.

Credits and acknowledgments borrowed from other sources and reproduced, with permission, in this textbook appear on appropriate page within text.

Pearson Education LTD.
Pearson Education Singapore, Pte. Ltd
Pearson Education, Canada, Ltd
Pearson Education–Japan

Pearson Education Australia PTY, Limited
Pearson Education North Asia Ltd
Pearson Educación de Mexico, S.A. de C.V.
Pearson Education Malaysia, Pte. Ltd

10 9 8 7 6 5 4 3 2 1

ISBN 0-13-142387-8

CONTENTS

Preface   xi

Acknowledgments   xiii

About the Authors   xv

CHAPTER 1   The Structure of Corporations   1

Forms of Business Ownership   2

People in Business   3

Separation of Ownership and Control   4

Can Investors Influence Managers?   5

Are Investors Helpless?   6

An Integrated System of Governance   7

International Monitoring   8

Summary   9

Questions   9

Endnotes   10

CHAPTER 2   Executive Incentives   11

Types of Executive Compensation   11

Base Salary and Bonus   12

Stock Options   12

Options and Accounting   13

Stock Options and (Mis)Alignment   14

Other Compensation   17

CEO Compensation Around the World   18

Summary   19

Questions   19

Exercises   19

Endnotes   20

CHAPTER 3   Accounting and Audits   21

Accounting Functions   21

Auditing   23

The Changing Role of Accounting   24

Consultants   27

An International Perspective 28

Summary 28

Questions 29

Exercises 29

Endnotes 29

CHAPTER 4 The Board of Directors 31

Historical Perspective 32

More Attention on Directors 32

Board Regulations 34

Who Are Directors? 35

Problems with Boards 35

Summary 39

Questions 39

Exercises 39

Endnotes 40

CHAPTER 5 Investment Banks 41

Some Historical Perspective 42

Investment Banking Activities 43

Investment Bank Criticisms 46

IPO Problems 46

Structured Deals 47

Summary 49

Questions 49

Exercises 49

Endnotes 50

CHAPTER 6 Financial Analysts 51

The Traditional Role of the Analyst 52

Quality of Recommendations 53

Analyst Compensation 54

Potential Conflicts of Interest 55

Analysts at Investment Banks 56

Just Who Is the Client? 57

Changing Roles 58

Summary 58

Questions 59

Exercises 59

Endnotes 59

CHAPTER 7   Credit Rating Agencies   61

A Brief Historical Perspective   61

The Ratings   63

Criticisms   64

Summary   67

Questions   67

Exercises   68

Endnotes   68

CHAPTER 8   The Securities and Exchange Commission   69

The Securities Acts   70

Organizational Structure of the SEC   71

Need for the Acts and the SEC   72

SEC Problem Areas   73

Summary   75

Questions   76

Exercises   76

Endnotes   76

CHAPTER 9   Shareholder Activism   78

What Is Shareholder Activism?   79

Does Institutional Shareholder Activism Work?   82

Potential Roadblocks to Effective Shareholder Activism   83

Summary   85

Questions   86

Exercises   86

Endnotes   86

Index   89

A decade ago, the term *corporate governance* was largely academic jargon. Today, the term is familiar to almost everyone. Unfortunately, its familiarity in our society comes about because revelations and news of corporate misdeeds have become a part of our daily lives. Enron and WorldCom, to give two well-known examples, engaged in misdeeds that led to their eventual downfall. Along the way, many shareholders lost their wealth and thus their faith and trust in corporate America. Why weren't these and other firms monitored more closely? Why did the managers misbehave? Why weren't their actions caught earlier by the boards of directors or by the auditors? Why didn't financial analysts and credit agencies warn the public? Where were the regulators? Now, everyone from mistrusting shareholders to bandwagon-jumping politicians is calling for better ways to monitor corporate America.

Why is corporate governance important? The goal of every firm is to increase its shareholders' wealth. However, the firm's value diminishes when it does not have the trust of its shareholders. *The entire economy suffers when trust is broken.* Effective corporate governance can instill confidence, and thus trust, in our companies and markets.

Believe it or not, we already have an extensive system of corporate governance. The system has never been perfect, but we have only begun to notice it. Now, the media regularly discusses corporate governance, and it is also discussed in every business school around the world.

INTENDED MARKET

This textbook, the first of its kind, provides an overview of our corporate governance system. The textbook can be used as an important supplement for (a) any corporate finance class, (b) an accounting class, (c) a variety of management classes, such as strategy, ethics, and/or especially business and society, and (d) a business law class. It is appropriate for both the undergraduate and graduate levels.

In addition, this text is sufficiently self-contained to be used as the sole text in an MBA module specifically focusing on corporate governance. The book can also be used for executive training programs and to this end can serve as an important reference for executive and academic libraries.

ORGANIZATION AND APPROACH OF THE TEXT

The text begins with an overview of the U.S. corporation. In the first chapter, we lay out the reasons why effective corporate governance is needed. In general, we believe that there are eight basic ways in which corporations can be effectively monitored. As such, after the first chapter, the rest of the book is organized into eight chapters. Every chapter is organized in the same way, and each chapter is self-contained. Chapters begin with a detailed overview of the monitor or monitoring mechanism and then highlight potential problems. Real-world examples are used to illustrate these problems. At the end of each chapter, we provide **Questions** that are based on the chapter reading, and we also offer **Exercises** that students can do to further their understanding of the chapter material.

While this textbook can be used in many ways in the classroom, one that works well is to use the contents of one or two chapters as the basis of discussions in a seminar-style format, where the instructor serves as facilitator. Outside class, students can subsequently work on **Exercises** based on those chapters and use them for the basis of discussions for the next class meeting, at which they serve as facilitators.

We hope you enjoy the book as much as we enjoyed writing it. If you have any suggestions or comments, we would be more than happy to receive them. You can e-mail Ken Kim at *kk52@buffalo.edu* or John Nofsinger at *john.nofsinger@cbe. wsu.edu* .

ACKNOWLEDGMENTS

This book could not have been written without the guidance and support that we have received from many people throughout our careers. We will not name names (in order to protect the innocent), but we wish to thank our former finance teachers for initially introducing us to the world of finance. We are also grateful to our former and current academic collaborators and to our former professional colleagues (especially the gang at the SEC) for shaping our way of thinking with regard to corporate governance. The reviewers of this book were so knowledgeable and insightful that we must make an exception to our own rule and give thanks to Tim Michael at James Madison University, Betty Simkins of Oklahoma State University, and Melissa Williams of the University of Houston—Clear Lake. We also readily acknowledge our friends who work on the front lines (i.e., in the "real world") and keep us grounded in reality, thus preventing us from getting carried away with our theories. We appreciate our publisher, Prentice Hall, for taking the risk and giving us the chance to produce this text, and its trade book division, Financial Times/Prentice Hall, for allowing us to draw liberally from our trade book, *Infectious Greed*. Finally, we are deeply indebted to our close friends and family for their support. They help us maintain our sanity.

Kenneth A. Kim, Ph.D., is a finance professor at the State University of New York (SUNY) at Buffalo. His research interests include corporate finance, corporate governance, and behavioral finance. His work has been published in the *Journal of Finance*, the *Journal of Business*, the *Journal of Corporate Finance*, and the *Journal of Banking and Finance*, as well as in other leading journals. He is coauthor of *Infectious Greed* (Financial Times Prentice Hall) and the textbook *Global Corporate Finance*. During 1998 and 1999, Kim worked as a financial economist at the U.S. Securities and Exchange Commission (SEC) in Washington, DC, where he worked on a wide variety of corporate finance issues, including mergers and acquisitions regulations. Kim regularly serves as a consultant to the Kuala Lumpur Stock Exchange. He has won awards for his teaching and has held a variety of academic posts at institutions around the world, including in Ecuador, Hong Kong, Japan, Korea, and Thailand.

John R. Nofsinger, Ph D., is a finance professor at Washington State University and author of *Investment Madness, The Psychology of Investing, Investment Blunders*, and coauthor of *Infectious Greed*. Widely acknowledged as one of the world's leading experts in investor psychology and behavioral finance, he is frequently quoted in financial media including *The Wall Street Journal, Fortune, Business Week, SmartMoney, Bloomberg*, and *CNBC*, as well as other media from the *Washington Post* to *Wired.com*. Nofsinger has published more than 20 articles in leading scholarly and professional journals. His research has won awards at the Financial Management Association, Chicago Quantitative Alliance, and PACAP conferences. He has also done advanced research for the New York Stock Exchange and the Association for Investment Management and Research.

The Structure of Corporations

Capitalism is an economic system of business based on private enterprise. Individuals and businesses own land, farms, factories, and equipment, and they use those assets in an attempt to earn profits. Capitalism is a good economic system because it can provide rewards for those who work hard and who are inventive and creative enough to figure out new or better products and services. One potential reward for creating value in an economy is the accumulation of personal wealth. The wealth incentive provides the fuel to generate new ideas and to foster economic value that provides jobs and raises our standard of living.

The main goal of a company is to create an environment conducive to earning long-term profits, which stem from two main sources. First, a business must provide products and/or services to a customer base. A large portion of a firm's value derives from the current and future profits of its business activity. Finding ways to increase profits from core operations can increase economic value. Second, increased profits can come from a growth in the sales of an existing product or sales resulting from the introduction of a new product.

Expansion usually requires additional money, or capital. Business activities also entail risk. The abilities to access capital and to control risk are important in the success or failure of a firm. Access to capital and the ability to control risks are influenced by the manner in which a firm is organized: A business can be a sole proprietorship, a partnership, or a corporation. Each organizational form involves different advantages and disadvantages.

FORMS OF BUSINESS OWNERSHIP

The first business form, a sole proprietorship, is owned by a single person. These businesses are relatively easy to start up and business tax is computed at the personal level. Due to its simplicity, sole proprietorships are ubiquitous, representing more than 70 percent of all U.S. businesses.[1] However, there are several significant drawbacks. Such firms often have a limited lifespan (they die with the owner's death or retirement), they have a limited ability to obtain capital, and the owner bears unlimited personal liability for the firm.

The second form is a partnership, which is similar to a sole proprietorship but there is more than one owner. As such, a partnership shares the advantages and disadvantages of the sole proprietorship. While one obvious advantage of a partnership is the ability to pool capital, this advantage may not be as important as combining service-oriented expertise and skill, especially for larger partnerships. Examples of such partnerships include accounting firms, law firms, investment banks, and advertising firms.

This text focuses on the third business form, the corporation. Fewer than 20 percent of all U.S. businesses are corporations but they generate approximately 90 percent of the country's business revenue.[2] The corporation is its own legal entity, as if it were a person. For example, the corporation can engage in business transactions and other business activities in its own name. Corporate officers act as agents for the firm and authorize those activities.

The biggest advantage of the corporate business form is access to capital markets. Public companies can raise money by issuing stocks and bonds to investors. While sole proprietorships and partnerships may access millions of dollars through the business owners' wealth and through banks, corporations may eventually access billions of dollars. Access to this capital causes entrepreneurs like Bill Gates of Microsoft, Steve Jobs of Apple, and Larry Ellison of Oracle to take their companies public. To raise money for expansion in the capital markets, the business sells stock to investors.

For example, between 1977 and 1980, Apple Computer sold a total of 121,000 computers. To meet the potential demand for millions of computers per year, Apple needed to expand operations significantly. As a result, in 1980 Apple became a public corporation and sold $65 million worth of stock. Steve Jobs, cofounder of Apple, still owned more shares than anyone else, but he owned less than half of the firm. He gave up a great deal of ownership to new investors in exchange for the capital to expand the firm. (Incidentally, as we will describe later, this decision would later come back to haunt Jobs.)

Stockholders, or shareholders, are the owners of a public corporation. These shareholders receive any value that is created by the firm, but they can also lose their investments if the firm goes bankrupt. The process has two benefits. First, any individual, as long as she or he has some money, can invest in business and increase their wealth over the long term. Second, businesses with growth potential can obtain capital needed to expand, which creates economic value, jobs, and taxes. A corporation has an infinite life unless terminated by bankruptcy or merger with another firm. The owners of corporations enjoy limited financial liability because they can lose only, at most, the value of their ownership shares. Further, corporate ownership is usually quite liquid, and ownership stakes can be easily bought and sold as stocks in a marketplace such as the New York Stock Exchange (NYSE) or Nasdaq.

The advantages of the corporate business form are appealing, but there are also major disadvantages. Corporate profits are subject to business taxes before any income goes to shareholders in the form of dividends. Subsequently, shareholders must also pay personal taxes on dividend income. Therefore, shareholders are exposed to double taxation. In addition, running a corporation can be quite expensive. For example, the costs of hiring accountants and legal experts, the costs of communicating with all shareholders, the costs of complying with regulations, and so forth, can cost millions of dollars per year. Finally, and perhaps the most important disadvantage, corporations suffer from potentially serious governance problems. Most investors only own a small stake of a large public corporation, and they consequently do not feel any true sense of ownership, or control, over the firms in which they own stock, as they would for a sole proprietorship or partnership.

PEOPLE IN BUSINESS

There are four groups of people involved with a public corporation: the shareholders, directors, officers, and employees. Shareholders literally own a public firm. As owners, they capture the economic value of the firm in the form of stock price increases and dividends, and they also suffer the losses when a firm fails. Directors hire, oversee, evaluate, and fire the officers of the firm. In doing so, they are supposed to represent the interests of the shareholders. The officers, such as the chief executive officer (CEO) and/or president, represent the firm's top level of management, and they are ultimately responsible for the day-to-day operation of the firm. Employees have a stake in the firm because they dedicate their human capital, i.e., their labor, to the firm; they may also be owners by holding company stock in their retirement plans.

The firm has other stakeholders as well, including creditors, government, suppliers, and customers, but these should be thought of as those who *deal* with the firm, rather than as an explicit part of the firm.

Given the number of people involved with the company, who actually controls the corporation? Who makes the crucial decisions and has the most power? One might think that the owners control the firm, or that the board of directors, who hire the officers, might have the control. However, for the most part, the officers control the firm.

SEPARATION OF OWNERSHIP AND CONTROL

Corporate ownership and control are divided between two parties—stockholders and officers. The stockholders own the firm and officers (or executives) control the firm. This situation comes about because the thousands, or even hundreds of thousands, of investors who own public firms could not collectively make the daily decisions needed to operate a business. Firms hire managers for that work.

Most shareholders do not wish to take part in a firm's business activities. These shareholders act like investors not owners. The difference is subtle, but important. Owners focus on the business performance of the firm and investors focus on the risk and return of their stock portfolios. While diversifying reduces risk for the investor, ownership of many companies also makes participation and influence in those companies less likely. Therefore, investors tend to be inactive shareholders of many firms.

There is a problem with this separation of ownership and control. Why would the managers care about the owners? It is not far-fetched to imagine that managers may act in their own personal interest if possible, even at the expense of owners. In academic terms, this situation is known as the principal-agent problem or the agency problem.

Consider the owner of a nightclub (the principal) who hires a bouncer (the agent) to check identification at the front door and to receive the cover charge from entering customers. The bouncer may pocket some of the cash if he thinks no one is looking and try to maximize his own wealth at the expense of the owner. If the owner cannot effectively monitor the transactions and the activities of the bouncer, he or she could lose money. Therefore, monitoring is important to help overcome the agency problem.

The shareholders of a corporation are the principals, and the managers who run the company are the agents. If shareholders cannot effectively monitor the managers' behavior, then managers may be tempted to use the firm's assets for their own ends, such as improving their lifestyles. Executives may enjoy perks such as liberally charging the corporate expense account, chartering the company jet, ordering top-grade office furniture, and so on, all at the expense of shareholders.

Solutions to this problem tend to come in two categories, incentives and monitoring. The incentive solution is to tie the wealth of the executive to the wealth of the shareholders, so that executives and shareholders want the same thing. This is called aligning executive incentives with shareholder desires. Managers would then act and behave in a way that is also best for the other shareholders. How can this be done? For most U.S. companies, executives are given stock, stock options, or both as a significant component of their compensation. The advantages and disadvantages of this incentive solution are explored in the next chapter. Suffice it to say, there are problems.

The second solution is to set up mechanisms for monitoring the behavior of managers. Indeed, several monitoring mechanisms are discussed below.

CAN INVESTORS INFLUENCE MANAGERS?

Theoretically, managers work for owners (shareholders). In reality, because shareholders are usually inactive, the firm actually seems to belong to management. Some active shareholders have tried to influence management, but they have often met defeat. Recent evidence of unsuccessful outcomes of shareholder proposals is quite telling. Shareholders have the power to make proposals that can be voted on at the annual shareholders meeting. There are generally two types of proposals, those related to governance (e.g., suggesting changes in board structure) and those oriented to social reform (e.g., proposing to stop selling chemicals to rogue countries). About half of all shareholder-initiated proposals progress far enough in the process to reach the voting stage. When there is a vote, such proposals usually are defeated.[3]

A huge factor in whether a proposal is successful depends on management's opinion. Without management approval, proposals have little chance of succeeding. Traditionally, shareholders have trusted management to know what is best for the firm. Most shareholders will go along with whatever management wants.

BOX 1-1

EXAMPLE–HEWLETT-PACKARD AND COMPAQ

For an illustration of management control and influence, consider the 2002 merger between Hewlett-Packard (HP) and Compaq.[4] Carly Fiorina, the Hewlett-Packard CEO, announced on September 4, 2001, that HP would acquire Compaq for $25.5 billion. The stock markets, industry experts, and the business media reacted negatively to the news. Hewlett-Packard stock was down 18 percent following the announcement, and even Compaq's stock declined by 10 percent, which is very rare for a target firm. Of particular note, David W. Packard and Walter Hewlett, both significant shareholders (when including the Packard Foundation, the pair owned 18 percent of HP stock) and sons of HP's founders, were also strongly opposed to the acquisition. In fact, they took out newspaper ads asking other HP shareholders to vote against the merger.

However, Fiorina went ahead with her plan, despite attacks from both Packard and Hewlett, and on March 19, 2002, most of the other shareholders voted in favor of the acquisition. Despite the controversy and the drop in stock prices, most shareholders voted with management's wishes and approved the acquisition. This example reinforces the idea that even though some investors may want to influence business strategy and direction, management controls the firm.

ARE INVESTORS HELPLESS?

Generally speaking, the investing public does not know what goes on at the firm's operational level. Managers handle day-to-day operations, and they know that their work is mostly unknown to investors. Consequently, managers may not act in the shareholder's best interest, which demonstrates the need for monitors.

Figure 1.1 illustrates the separation of ownership and control between stockholders and managers. In addition, the figure shows that monitors exist inside the corporate structure, outside the structure, and in government.

The monitors inside a public firm are the board of directors who oversee management and are supposed to represent shareholders' interests. The board evaluates management and can also design compensation contracts to tie management's salaries to the firm's performance. You may remember that Apple Computer was cofounded by Steve Jobs. When the firm became a public corporation, Jobs was the largest shareholder, and he also became CEO. However, the Apple board of directors felt that Jobs was not experienced enough to steer the firm through its rapid expansion. Therefore, they hired John Sculley as CEO in 1983. In 1985, a power struggle ensued for control of the firm, and the board backed Sculley. Jobs was forced out of Apple and no longer had a say in business operations even though he was the largest shareholder. (Interestingly, when Apple Computer experienced difficulties in the late 1990s, the board hired Jobs back as CEO!)

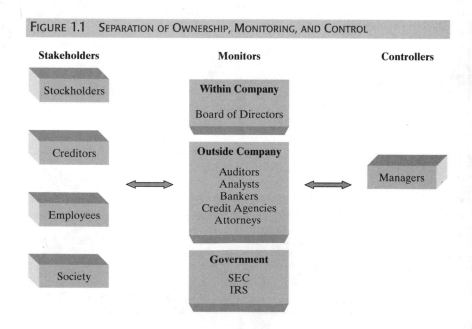

FIGURE 1.1 SEPARATION OF OWNERSHIP, MONITORING, AND CONTROL

Stakeholders	Monitors	Controllers
Stockholders	**Within Company** Board of Directors	
Creditors	**Outside Company** Auditors Analysts Bankers Credit Agencies Attorneys	Managers
Employees		
Society	**Government** SEC IRS	

As shown in the figure, outsiders—including auditors, analysts, banks, credit rating agencies, and outside legal counsel—all interact with the firm and monitor manager activities. Auditors examine the firm's accounting systems and comment on whether financial statements fairly represent the financial position of the firm. Investors and other stakeholders use the public financial statements to make decisions about the firm's financial health, prospects, performance, and value. Even though investors may not have the ability or opportunity to validate the firm's activities, accountants and auditors can attest to the firm's financial health and verify its activities.

Investment analysts who follow a firm conduct their own, independent evaluations of the company's business activities and report their findings to the investment community. Analysts are supposed to give unbiased and expert assessments.

Investment banks also interact with management by helping firms access the capital markets. When obtaining more capital from public investors, firms must register documents with regulators that show potential investors the condition of the firm. Investment banks help firms with this process and advise managers on how to interact with the capital markets.

The government also monitors business activities through the Securities and Exchange Commission (SEC) and the Internal Revenue Service (IRS). The SEC regulates public firms for the protection of public investors, and it makes policy and prosecutes violators in civil court. However, for criminal prosecution the SEC must turn to the U.S. Justice Department. The IRS enforces the tax rules to ensure corporations pay taxes, just as it does with individual American citizens.

As a group, this is a pretty impressive set of monitors. Unfortunately, all of these mechanisms can fail at one time or another. An important purpose of this text is to describe each of these corporate monitors and the problems that may exist with each of them.

AN INTEGRATED SYSTEM OF GOVERNANCE

The corporate governance system is integrated and complicated. The potential incentives for executives, auditors, boards, banks, and so on, to misbehave are intertwined. By focusing on one part of the system, readers might not fully understand how the governance system can break down. Consider the diagram of corporate participants in Figure 1.2. The arrows show the relationships between the groups. Note that these relationships are interconnected.

For example, analysts talk to management to gauge the prospects of the firm. Managers want to paint a rosy picture so that analysts will recommend a "buy" rating and the stock price will rise. However, this situation may also cause analysts to predict a high profit forecast for the company, and the managers may struggle to meet the high forecast. If the business activities of the firm do not

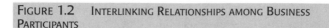

FIGURE 1.2   INTERLINKING RELATIONSHIPS AMONG BUSINESS PARTICIPANTS

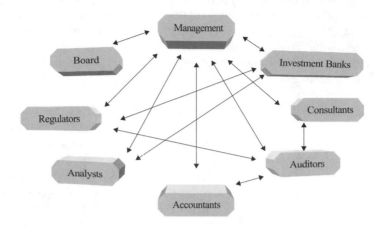

merit the high profit forecast, managers might then pressure their accounting department to help. In some cases, consultants are hired who recommend aggressive accounting techniques to help show increased profits.

The public auditors for the firm may have had a long and fruitful relationship with the company, auditing the books for many years. The auditors are proud to have a prestigious corporation as a client and do not want to end this relationship; consequently they may not press too hard on limiting aggressive accounting methods. This circumstance holds true especially if the consultants who recommended those methods are from the auditors' own accounting and auditing firm.

Why are managers so obsessed with pushing hard for smooth and increasing profits? Why are they obsessed with gaining analyst favor? It is because a board (which is largely picked by the managers) awards them stock options and stock incentives. If managers can increase the price of the stock, then they can cash in their options and stock and become rich.

Regulators also monitor managers' behavior. However, regulators often have experience as partners in consulting firms, auditing firms, or law firms that are an integral part of the system. By participating in the corporate system, regulators know how it works. Unfortunately, they might also have their own conflicts of interest.

INTERNATIONAL MONITORING

Other capitalist countries use the types of monitoring and incentives used in the United States to align the interests of executives and shareholders. However, important differences do occur. In many countries, laws, regulation, and enforcement are considerably more lax than in the United States. For example, Japan's version of the SEC is the Securities and Exchange Surveillance Commission (SESC). The SESC has only one-tenth the number of SEC employees, and the SEC is already considered to be grossly understaffed.[5] The SESC does not even have the power to file civil suits or bring administrative action against market participants. The securities regulator in Taiwan, the Securities and Futures Commission, also does not have the authority to conduct investigations; instead, they must rely on local prosecutors who have little experience with the market and with accounting fraud. In addition, in 2001 in Italy, the charge of false accounting was reduced to a mere misdemeanor.

The tale of Germany's Gerhard Schmid, the former CEO of MobilCom, is telling. As CEO, in 2001, Schmid transferred €70.9 million ($69.5 million) in new MobilCom stock to a shell company his wife controlled. The German regulatory group, the German Financial Supervisory Authority, said that the actions did not fall under their jurisdiction. Consequently, there was no investigation, even though Schmid broke German law by not informing other executives or the board. The firm's board of directors did find out about the transfer and investigated. In June 2002, the board fired Schmid and demanded the return of the money. In most countries, the laws, regulators, and enforcement are so weak that corporate fraud conviction is unlikely.

❖ SUMMARY

The corporate form of business allows firms that need capital to obtain it and expand, thereby helping the economy. This form also allows people with money to provide those funds and profit from having ownership in business. The disadvantage of public corporations lies in the relation between ownership and control. Managers who control the firm can take advantage of the investors who own the firm. To inhibit poor managerial behavior, shareholders try to align the executives' interests with their own interests through incentive programs involving stock and stock options. In addition, the corporate system has several different groups of people that monitor managers. Unfortunately, both alignment incentives and monitoring groups have problems. The corporate system has interrelated incentives that combine to create an environment where people can act unethically. The following chapters discuss each aspect of the incentive and monitor system.

QUESTIONS

1. How can executive compensation align manager interests with shareholder interests?
2. Name and describe the different groups that monitor a firm.
3. Describe the separation of ownership and control. Explain how that separation comes about and why it leads to problems.
4. Compare and contrast the participants in the U.S. corporate governance system with those in other countries.

ENDNOTES

1. William J. Megginson, *Corporate Finance Theory* (Reading, MA: Addison-Wesley, 1997), p. 40.
2. Ibid.
3. See, for example, Stuart Gillan and Laura Starks, "A Survey of Shareholder Activism: Motivation and Empirical Evidence," *Contemporary Finance Digest* 2, no. 3 (1998):10–34; Cynthia Campbell, Stuart Gillan, and Cathy Niden, "Current Perspectives on Shareholder Proposals: Lessons from the 1997 Proxy Season," *Financial Management* 28, no. 1 (1999):89–98; and Gordon and Pound, "Information, Ownership Structure, and Shareholder Voting: Evidence from Shareholder-Sponsored Corporate Governance Proposals," *Journal of Finance* 47, no. 2 (1993):697–718.
4. Larry Magid, "Many Would Lose in Hewlett-Packard, Compaq Merger," *Los Angeles Times*, *www.larrysworld.com/articles/synd.hp merger.htm*: Mike Elgan and Susan B. Shor, "Gloves Are Off in Merger Fight," *HP World* 5, no. 2, *www.interex.org/hpworldnews/hpw202/01news.html*.
5. Almar Latour and Kevin Delaney, "Outside the U.S., Executives Face Little Legal Peril," *The Wall Street Journal*, August 16, 2002, A1.

EXECUTIVE INCENTIVES

A corporation's ownership and control are separated between two parties—stockholders and officers. The stockholders own the firm, and officers (or executives) control the firm. A simple problem exists with this separation of ownership and control. Why should the managers care about the owners? Managers may put personal interests first, even at the expense of owners This situation is known as the principal-agent problem or the agency problem. The shareholders of a corporation are the principals and the managers who run the company are the agents. If shareholders cannot effectively monitor managers' behavior, then the latter may be tempted to use the firm's assets to enhance their own lifestyles.

Solutions to agency problems tend to fall in two categories: incentives and monitoring. The board of directors, auditors, and other components of the governance system serve to monitor managers; this is discussed in later chapters. The incentive solution, covered in this chapter, ties an executive's wealth to the wealth of shareholders so that everyone shares the same goal. This is called aligning executive incentives with shareholders' desires. Managers should then act in ways that also benefit other shareholders. To align manager and shareholder interests, most executives receive stock and/or stock options as a significant component of their compensation. In this chapter, we focus on the incentives of modern executive compensation.

TYPES OF EXECUTIVE COMPENSATION

Company executives are compensated in many different ways. They receive a basic salary that also includes pension contributions and perquisites (company car, club memberships, and so on). In addition, top executives might receive a bonus that is usually linked to accounting-based performance measures. Lastly, managers might receive additional wealth through long-term incentive programs, usually in the form of stock options, which reward the manager for increasing the company's stock price. Stock grants are another common form of long-term awards.

BASE SALARY AND BONUS

The base salary of a company CEO is often determined through the benchmarking method, which surveys peer CEO salaries for comparison.[1] Salaries less than the 50th percentile are considered under market, while salaries in the 50th to 75th percentile are competitive. CEO base salary has continuously drifted upward because CEOs typically argue for competitive salaries. Interestingly, this basic pay results more from characteristics of the firm (for example, industry, size) than on characteristics of the CEO (for example, age, experience). In recent years, the average base salary has been about $500,000. The salary at a large company can be much higher. Benchmarking also occurs for bonus and option programs.

At the end of every year, the CEO receives a cash bonus. The size of the payment is based on the performance of the firm over the past year, and it typically is based on the accounting profit measurements of EPS (earnings per share) and EBIT (earnings before interest and taxes). Measures of economic value added (or EVA) are also common. These value-added measures are usually variations on earnings minus the cost of capital. The idea is to measure the value added to the firm in relation to the firm's costs of using different sources of money to conduct its business activities. Whether EBIT or EVA is used, a low threshold needs to be reached in order to qualify the CEO for a bonus. Higher levels of firm performance merit higher bonus amounts, up to a specific maximum, or cap.

The use of accounting profits to measure performance has several potential drawbacks. First, to boost accounting profits, a CEO has an incentive to forego costly research and development that might make the firm more profitable in the future than in the present. Second, accounting profits may be manipulated (see the next chapter). Third, the bonus plan is developed anew each year, and if the threshold cannot be met one year, the CEO has an incentive to move earnings from the present year to the future. This would lower expectations while the next year's bonus plan is being created and artificially increase the executive's chance of receiving that bonus. In short, CEOs may place too much focus on manipulating short-term earnings instead of focusing on long-term earnings and shareholder wealth. The average bonus payment has been about $250,000 in recent years.

STOCK OPTIONS

Executive stock options are the most common form of market-oriented incentive pay. Stock options are contracts that allow executives to buy shares of stock at a

fixed price, called the exercise or strike price. Therefore, if the price o
rises above the strike price, the executive will capture the difference as a proht.
For example, if the stock of a company trades at $50 per share, the CEO may be
given options with a strike price at $50. Over the next few years, if the stock price
rises to $75 per share, then shareholders would receive a 50 percent return on
their stockholdings. The CEO could buy stock for $50 per share by exercising the
option and sell it for $75 per share, thus making a $25 profit on each option
owned. If the executive has options for 1 million shares, then he or she could
pocket $25 million. If the stock price reaches $100 per share, the executive could
cash in for $50 million. In contrast, if the stock price were to drop to less than $50
per share then the options have no exercisable value and are said to be underwater. Executives treat stock options as compensation; they nearly always exercise
the options to buy the stock and then sell the stock for the cash. Only rarely will
an executive keep the stock.

   Stock options give the executives of the firm the incentive to manage the firm
in such a way that the stock price increases, which is precisely what the stockholders want as well. Therefore, stock options are believed to align managers' goals with
shareholders' goals. This alignment helps to overcome some of the problems with
the separation of ownership and control. The typical executive option contract
assigns the strike price of the options to the prevailing stock price when the option
is granted. The most common length of the options contract is 10 years. That is, the
CEO has 10 years to increase the price of the stock and exercise the options. After
10 years, the options expire. Executives cannot sell or transfer their options and are
discouraged from hedging the stock price risk. The average incentive award real-
ized, mostly through stock options, jumped from $500,000 in 2000 to more than
$800,000 in 2001. Executive stock options were not common prior to 1980.

OPTIONS AND ACCOUNTING

The popularity of stock options as incentive compensation in the United States
partly comes from its very favorable tax treatment for both the executive and the
company. When options are granted, the company only needs to report an
accounting cost when the strike price is less than the current stock price. Then the
cost is amortized over the life of the option. Because most options are granted
with the strike price equal to the current stock price, the firm never has to report
an accounting cost. Of course, there is an economic cost to the firm, but that is not
reported in the current generally accepted accounting principles (GAAP). Also,
the manager can pick the year in which he or she will exercise the options and
thus determine when the tax liability occurs. In addition, the compensation is
treated as a capital gain, not as income, which is an advantage to the CEO
because capital gains taxes are lower than regular personal income taxes.

   The current use of options and GAAP reporting standards usually make the cost
of options non-reportable in the income statement. That is, if an executive cashes in
for $100 million, this cost does not appear on the firm's income statement; the firm
does not have to report an accounting cost. However, the economic cost to the firm is

real. Consider this simple example. A firm has 100 million shares outstanding and has given the executives options for 10 million shares. The firm currently has earnings of $100 million, or $1 per share. If the executives exercise their options, then they would buy 10 million shares from the firm at the strike price and sell them on the stock market. At that point, there would be 110 million shares outstanding, which means that the $100 million in earnings becomes only $0.91 per share. The earnings per share have fallen by 9 percent, and the firm has become less profitable to its shareholders.

STOCK OPTIONS AND (MIS)ALIGNMENT

Despite the tremendous growth in the use of stock options as incentive compensation for executives, very little direct evidence exists that they work. That is, when managers are awarded stock options, do their firms and its stock perform better, on average? Financial economists have studied this question for at least two decades. The evidence is mixed. One study identifies a positive relationship between executive stock incentives and firm performance, but another controls for other corporate monitoring mechanisms (such as capital structure, board structure, institutional owners, and so on) and finds no relation between stock-based incentives and firm performance.[2] There remains little direct evidence that a company can expect higher stock returns by introducing aggressive incentive-based compensation programs.

Stock options may not be as effective in aligning managerial incentives with shareholder goals as once thought. The following list cites improperly aligned incentives involving options.

1. Shareholder returns combine both stock price appreciation and dividends. The stock option is only affected by price appreciation. Therefore, the CEO might forego increasing dividends in favor of using the cash to try to increase the stock price.
2. The stock price is more likely to increase when the CEO accepts risky projects. Therefore, when a firm uses options to compensate the CEO, he or she has a tendency to pick a higher risk business strategy.
3. Stock options lose some incentive for the CEO if the stock price falls too far below the strike price. In this case, the options would be too far underwater to motivate the manager effectively.
4. Stock analysts and investors focus a great deal on a firm's accounting profits, and the firm often has some ability to manipulate earnings. As a result, the CEO may have an incentive to manipulate earnings and thus maximize profits in one target year to make the stock price more favorable for exercising options. This manipulation can reduce earnings (and consequently the stock price) after the target year.

The very advantage that stock options have of aligning manager incentives with stockholder goals also constitutes a major problem. Stock options are tied to the firm's stock price, which helps align incentives, but executives only have partial influence on stock prices. Stock prices are affected by company performance but also by many other factors beyond control, particularly the strength or weakness of the economy. When the economy thrives, then stock prices rise. Even the stock price of a poorly run company may rise, although not as much as its more successful competitors. This occurrence may richly reward executives of poorly run firms through their options when they do not deserve them. Alternatively, the stock market may fall because of poor economic conditions or investor pessimism. A company whose management outperforms its competitors may still find that its stock is falling. In that case, managers should be rewarded, but they are not because their options go underwater when the market falls.

Options lose their effectiveness when the stock price falls far below the strike price. The stock price decline could be either related to a company's poor performance or to a general stock market decline. To reestablish motivation for the executives, boards sometimes reprice previously issued options and lower the strike price. Consider the incentives listed above and how they create interesting dynamics for CEO behavior. Executives may choose risky company projects that have a chance of dramatically increasing the stock price. If the projects succeed, the CEO becomes rich and the stockholders experience increased wealth. However, if the projects fail, the stockholders lose money. Alternatively, the CEO simply asks the board to reprice the options and the CEO can then repeat the strategy. Proponents of option repricing claim that it is necessary to keep executives at the firm. This argument has some truth, but that does not change the skewed incentives it causes.

BOX 2-1

EXAMPLE–DISNEY

Using stock options can be a powerful way to align the interests of the managers and the shareholders. But is it an effective way? Consider the compensation of Disney CEO Michael Eisner and the value creation at Disney. Eisner was given millions of stock options. If he could add substantial value to Disney, he could cash in for incredible wealth. Consider what he did in the five years starting in 1992. By 1997, Disney was earning three times the profits of 1992. Eisner had added more than $13 billion in value to the firm. The stock price more than doubled from $14.33 to $33.00.[3] Disney's stockholders benefited greatly from this value creation. So did Michael Eisner. His annual salary in 1997 was $750,000, and he received a $9.9 million bonus. He also cashed in $565 million in stock options, for a total compensation of $575.7 million.[4]

Unfortunately for Disney shareholders, the story doesn't end there. Over the next four years after 1997, Disney's profits struggled and the stock price suffered. In 2001, Disney lost $158 million and the stock price ended the year at only $20.72. Eisner received his $1 million salary, but he received no bonuses and did not exercise stock options.[5] Eisner's salary, and that of other Disney managers, has been closely tied to the performance of Disney's profits and stock price. These executives received much lower pay when Disney declined. However, the shareholders lost more than half of the value that was created before 1997. Yet Eisner maintained the incredible income he received for generating that stock price appreciation, even though much of it later disappeared. Most of that income came from Disney stock options.

Examples like that of Eisner and Disney are not fraudulent or illegal. Boards of directors freely give executives stock options and, therefore, create the possibility that only short-term value will be created, not long-term value. However, in other cases, managers seem to mislead the public in order to enrich themselves. Consider the management actions at Xerox Corporation.

BOX 2-2

EXAMPLE–XEROX CORPORATION

In a civil action by the SEC against Xerox, the SEC claimed senior management directed a scheme that improperly accelerated leasing operations revenue from 1997 to 2000. The accounting maneuvering increased revenue by $3 billion and profits by $1.5 billion over that period. In subsequent financial restatements, Xerox shifted out $6.4 billion of revenue for that time. The accounting actions violated generally accepted accounting practices and were not disclosed to shareholders or regulators. Xerox perpetrated the scheme to meet ever increasing internal and analyst earnings expectations, and it became common for Xerox executives to assign numerical goals to be produced through accounting gimmickry.[6] Indeed, both the chief financial officer (CFO) and vice chairman of Xerox, and the president of

FIGURE 2.1   XEROX STOCK PRICE FROM JANUARY 1990 TO JULY 2002

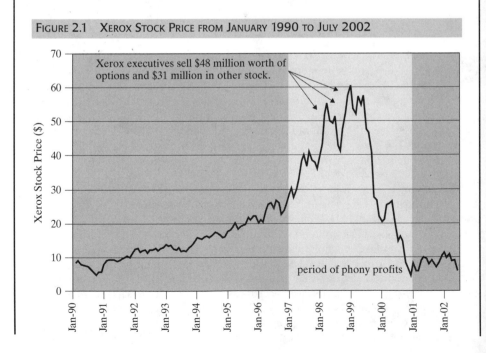

Xerox executives sell $48 million worth of options and $31 million in other stock.

period of phony profits

Xerox Europe believed that excluding accounting maneuvers, the firm had essentially no growth in the 1990s.[7]

The artificial profits helped drive the stock price from a split-adjusted $13 at the end of 1996 to more than $60 in 1999. During this time of inflated stock prices, Xerox CEO Paul Allaire sold stock and profited by $16 million. Xerox executives, in total, sold $79 million worth of stock between 1997 and 1999. Of the total, $48 million was from exercising stock options and the other $31 million was from stock sales. Figure 2.1 shows the relationship between the fraudulent reporting, the stock price, and the executive sales. In April 2002, Xerox admitted to the SEC that it had improperly recorded the earnings and agreed to pay a $10 million fine. Of course, the fine is paid by the firm, and thus is a cost to the victimized stockholders.[8] The stock price fell to less than $10 per share, approximately the price ten years earlier. While the firm has lost any value created in the 1990s, the managers received millions of dollars.

OTHER COMPENSATION

Executives often receive other forms of compensation that are sometimes not reported to the SEC on official documents. The old style perk of a company paying for a CEO's club membership may come to mind, but that is passé compared to modern perks. The company will frequently pay for financial advisors, luxury cars and chauffeurs, personal travel, Manhattan apartments, and more.

Retirement (or resignation) compensation is also popular. For example, when Terrence Murray, former CEO and current chairman of FleetBoston, retires, he will receive a pension payment of $5.8 million per year. In addition, he can use corporate jets for his travel (and that of his guests) for up to 150 hours per year.[9] Louis Gerstner retired as CEO of IBM (though he continued for a time as chairman) in March 2002. In addition to his $2 million yearly pension, he has access to corporate planes, cars, and apartments for 20 years. If IBM wants Gerstner's advice, he will be paid $600 per hour.[10]

Another benefit is obtaining a company loan. Executives commonly borrow hundreds of thousands, or even millions of dollars at extremely low interest rates—sometimes even interest free. These loans may be used to purchase expensive homes: Wells Fargo CEO Richard Kovacevich borrowed $1 million for a house down payment. The savings on low interest loans can quickly add up to tens or hundreds of thousands of dollars. Frequently, executives do not even pay back the loans. Mattel Corp. absolved ousted CEO Jill Barad from repaying a $7.2 million loan and then paid her an additional $3.3 million to cover the cost of resulting additional taxes.[11] The new CEO, Robert Eckert, received a $5.5 million loan and will not have to repay it if he stays with the firm for two years. A similar arrangement exists with Compaq Chairman and CEO Michael Capellas for his $5 million loan.

CEO COMPENSATION AROUND THE WORLD

Paying the top officer in the company with long-term incentive awards is most common in the United States. Figure 2.2 shows the total compensation of CEOs in the United States for 2000 and 2001. Also, 2001 CEO compensation in 17 foreign firms is shown. The data comes from surveys conducted by Towers Perrin.[12] The figure shows estimates of average CEO pay in firms with at least $500 million in sales. CEO compensation is reported as incentive awards (e.g., stock options) in addition to base salary and bonus pay.

The figure shows that both the base pay and incentive awards for U.S. companies grew substantially between 2000 and 2001. Total compensation for U.S. CEOs grew 38 percent from $1.4 million to $1.9 million. Base salaries in the United States have been increasing quickly.

Note that total compensation for U.S. CEOs is much higher than that of foreign CEOs. After the United States, the next highest total CEO compensation is in Argentina and Mexico, which averaged $879,000 and $866,000, respectively, for 2001. Note that this is less than half of the U.S. CEO compensation. Other notable countries shown are Canada ($787,000), Hong Kong ($736,500), Germany ($455,000), Japan ($508,000), Spain ($430,000), and the United

FIGURE 2.2   LEVELS OF CEO COMPENSATION AROUND THE WORLD

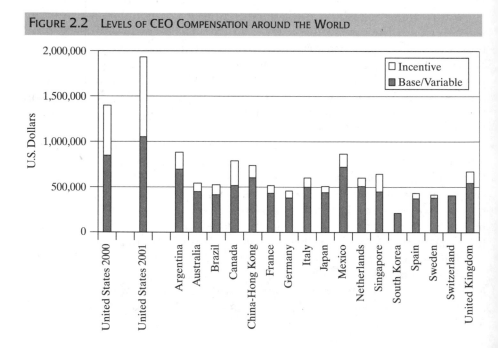

Kingdom ($668,500). Also note that the United States appears to use incentive awards such as stock options as compensation much more than other countries. In 2001, 45 percent of total compensation came in the form of incentive awards in the United States. The country with the next highest proportion of incentive pay to total pay is Canada, with 30 percent. South Korea and Switzerland use no material amounts of incentive awards.

❖ SUMMARY

The disadvantage of public corporations is the separation of ownership and control. Managers, who control the firm, can take advantage of investors, who own the firm. To inhibit poor managerial behavior, shareholders try to align the executive's interests with their own through incentive programs involving stocks and stock options. Managers, academics, and boards of directors have argued that stock and option incentives reduce this conflict between those who own the firm and those who control it. When executives work hard to increase the firm's stock price over the long term, both the shareholders and the executives reap the benefit.

However, stock options create an economic cost to the firm and sometimes do not create the correct rewards for good and poor managers. In addition, stock options also create other incentives that are not aligned with stockholder interests. For example, options create the incentive for managers to manipulate earnings and time the market with exercising those options.

QUESTIONS

1. What misalignments do stock options create?
2. When might options fail to reward good managers?
3. How does the repricing of stock options affect a manager's incentives?
4. How does executive pay in the United States compare to pay internationally?
5. List the pros and cons of compensating a CEO with stock options.

EXERCISES

1. Consider that a manager has already cashed in incentive compensation (like stock options) for tens, or hundreds, of millions of dollars. Does the awarding of more options still induce the alignment of interests? Why?
2. KPMG was the auditing firm for Xerox during the time it illegally manipulated its accounting figures (see the Xerox example). To what degree is KPMG to blame for fraud? Should it, like Xerox, be held accountable? What has the SEC done about KPMG's role?

3. The former CEO of Tyco, Dennis Kozlowski, has been accused of many abuses of the stockholder's money; describe some of these.
4. John, Tim, and Michael Rigas were arrested for perpetrating massive financial fraud and looting Adelphia Communications. Describe what happened.
5. Obtain the total compensation of five CEOs of companies (of different sizes and in different industries). Compare and contrast their compensation and comment on the potential alignment or misalignment of incentives.

ENDNOTES

1. Much of the compensation description in this section is summaries from Kevin Murphy, "Executive Compensation," in *Handbook of Labor Economics*, ed. O. Ashenfelter and D. Card, Vol. 3B. Amsterdam: North-Hollan Publishers, 1999.
2. See, for example, Hamid Mehran, "Executive Compensation Structure, Ownership, and Firm Performance," *Journal of Financial Economics* 38 (1995):163–184; and Charles Himmelberg, Glenn Hubbard, and Darius Palia, "Understanding the Determinants of Managerial Ownership and the Link Between Ownership and Performance," *Journal of Financial Economics* 53 (1999):353–384.
3. These are split-adjusted stock price figures.
4. Tim Smart, "An Eye-Popping Year for Executive Pay," *Washington Post*, March 22, 1998, H1.
5. Richard Verrier, "Eisner's Paycheck Humbled in 2001," *Los Angeles Times*, January 5, 2002, C1.
6. James Bandler and Mark Maremont, "Seeing Red: How Ex-Accountant

Added Up to Trouble for Humbled Xerox," *Wall Street Journal*, June 28, 2001, A1.
7. *SEC v. Xerox Corporation*, Civil Action No. 02-272789, Southern District of New York, U.S. District Court, (April 11, 2002).
8. Andrew Countryman, "Focus of Xerox Probe Shifts to Stock Sales," *Chicago Tribune*, July 2, 2002, 1.
9. Joann Lublin, "As CEOs' Reported Salaries and Bonuses Get Pinched, Many Chiefs Are Finding Hidden Ways to Increase Their Compensation," *Wall Street Journal*, April 11, 2002, B7.
10. Joann Lublin, "How CEOs Retire in Style," *Wall Street Journal*, September 13, 2002, B1.
11. Gary Strauss, "Many Execs Pocket Perks Aplenty," *USA Today*, May 1, 2001, B1.
12. Specifically, the data are from *2000 Worldwide Total Remuneration* and the *Worldwide Total Remuneration 2001–2002* studies by Towers Perrin.

ACCOUNTING AND AUDITS

Accountants and auditors are an important part of a corporate monitoring system. Indeed, auditors may be in the best position to monitor companies because the firm opens its books to them. In this process, auditors obtain private information about the company that others cannot obtain, and they use this information to determine whether the company's public financial statements reflect the true level of business being conducted. Banks, creditors, and others rely on these statements to provide an accurate picture of the firm's business activities and financial health. Investors use these public statements to assess the value of the company. Therefore, the auditor's candid evaluation of those statements is crucial. This chapter discusses the role of accountants and auditors as corporate monitors.

ACCOUNTING FUNCTIONS

Historically, accounting has been the function of gathering, compiling, reporting, and archiving a firm's business activities. This accounting information helps individuals in many roles who depend on it to make decisions. For convenience, those who need accounting information are categorized as either insiders or outsiders of the firm.

Management accounting is the development of information for insiders, i.e., company managers. Managers use this information to measure the progress toward their goals and highlight any potential problems in advance. For example, managers want to know which products have the best sales and which are selling poorly. Which products tend to sell together? How is inventory being managed? What about cash? Will the firm have enough cash to pay its upcoming debt payments?

Accountants answer these questions with budgets, variance reports, sensitivity analysis, revenue reports, cost projections, and even analysis of competitors. When firms consider how to expand products and services, managerial accountants help formulate profit projections from revenue and cost projections. In short, managerial accounting has historically played a big part in the control and evaluation of the business and its performance.

Outsiders of the firm also use accounting information. Investors, banks, the government, and other stakeholders have a keen interest in the financial health of the firm. Banks and other creditors want to know if the firm will be able to pay its debts. Shareholders want to know how profitable the firm is and how profitable it may be in the future. Employees might have a double interest because they have their careers and employment at stake, and they might be investors through their retirement plans as well.

Financial accounting provides information for outsiders. Whereas managerial accounting reports may break down performance for managers by individual products or regions of the country, financial reports summarize the business as a whole, although they can be broken into business segments and regions. In the case of publicly held companies, these reports are the quarterly and annual financial statements that they must file with the Securities and Exchange Commission (SEC).

The three main financial statements (income statement, balance sheet, and statement of cash flows) and other pieces of important information (e.g., popular press articles and analyst recommendations) are used by outsiders to determine the firm's value, profits, and its risk. Outsiders want to be able to compare firms easily. Thus, the SEC requires that these reports adhere to a uniform set of standards known as *generally accepted accounting principles* (GAAP) for public companies. These statements are prepared by the accountants of the firm and reviewed by independent accountants from an auditing firm (more on auditors later in the chapter).

The Internal Revenue Service (IRS) also requires accounting information, in this case for tax purposes. The accountants of the firm report profits or losses to the IRS and determine the tax bill. Interestingly, accounting methods and business record keeping can be very different for reports to managers, for public financial statements, and for the IRS. For example, there are ambiguities regarding how to record some transactions in GAAP. When reporting business activities in an annual report, choices are made that maximize earnings in order to make them appear stronger than they would be otherwise in hopes of driving up the firm's stock price. When IRS forms are being completed, choices are made to minimize earnings in order to minimize tax expenditures.[1]

A private-sector body, Financial Accounting Standards Board (FASB), sets the rules for financial statements. The SEC recognizes FASB as authoritative, which means that the SEC recognizes FASB decisions on creating and amending GAAP. However, the SEC and the U.S. Congress have been able to influence FASB accounting policies. Associations in the accounting profession sponsor FASB, and, to promote independence, its seven board members are required to serve full time and divest their interests in their former employers. Even non-CPAs serve on the FASB board.

AUDITING

Auditors are accountants from outside the firm who review the firm's financial statements and its procedures for producing them. Their job is to attest to the fairness of the statements and that they materially represent the condition of the firm. While banks and other creditors have always wanted independent verification of a firm's financial health, the role of monitoring a firm was cemented by the Securities Act of 1933 and the Securities Exchange Act of 1934. In the Great Depression, after the corporate spending excesses of the late 1920s, the country was reeling from business scandals. Congress reacted with legislation that called for stronger oversight and regulation and required annual independent audits of all public companies.

Because of this legislative requirement, in the late 1930s and 1940s accounting firms flourished with the increased demand for auditing services. Initially, the high demand resulted from the new laws that required independent verification of a firm's financial books. The demand for auditing services continued to grow as the economy eventually picked up and the number of public firms increased. There was plenty of business for auditing firms, and the environment was such that they could play an effective role as independent monitors—even becoming adversarial with the firm if necessary.

In the 1970s and 1980s, the auditing business began to change. The number of new companies that needed auditing services was no longer expanding. If auditing firms wanted to grow, they had to steal clients away from other auditing firms. The code of ethics was changed to permit advertising and other competitive practices. Auditing firms began to advertise and cut their prices to lure new clients. The relationship between the auditing firm and the audited company also began to change; with other audit firms courting them, corporate managers no longer tolerated adversarial auditors. Auditors became friendlier in order to keep their clients, especially the larger companies. Because of the prestige associated with having Fortune 500 companies as clients, auditing firms became less confrontational in order to keep them as clients. During this period, auditing firms also developed consulting services to advise companies on how to improve their accounting methods and business activities. This provided both another source of income for accounting firms and a way to solidify their relationships with company management.

THE CHANGING ROLE OF ACCOUNTING

During the last two decades the role of accounting departments within companies has changed. Instead of simply providing information to insiders and outsiders, accounting departments have begun to transition into being profit centers. Instead of simply reporting the quarterly profits of the firm, accounting departments are asked to increase profits through application of accounting methods. In some areas, the ambiguity in GAAP and the subjectivity of business activities provide for different ways of accounting for the same transaction. Different methods often lead to different levels of reportable profits.

One example of variations in accounting method applications relates to the desire of companies to exhibit a steady growth in profits. If the profits generated by business activities grow, but at an erratic pace, then accountants are asked to smooth out the earnings over time. This process is referred to as *managing earnings.*

BOX 3-1

EXAMPLE–GENERAL ELECTRIC

General Electric (GE) has been accused of using accounting manipulations to manage its earnings.[2] Notice in Figure 3.1 how steady the growth in GE's earnings has been,

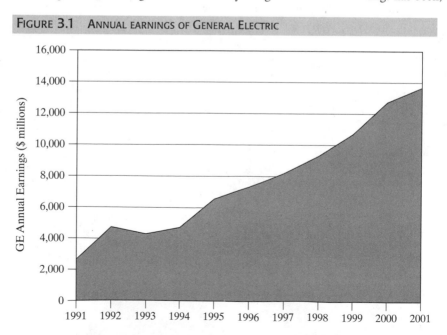

FIGURE 3.1   ANNUAL EARNINGS OF GENERAL ELECTRIC

especially since 1995. The accusations claim that GE employs a number of confusing but apparently legal gimmicks to achieve its consistent growth. For example, GE's financing division, GE Capital, can reduce current earnings for the firm by being pessimistic in its estimates of losses from problem loans. If those loans eventually are repaid, future profits will increase. The maneuver effectively shifts some earnings into the future. If the firm is in need of more earnings in the present, it can conduct a real estate sale and leaseback. The transaction could work like this. General Electric sells a factory to investors for $100 million. GE signs a long-term lease with the investors so that GE still uses the factory. However, because the factory has been depreciated to $50 million, GE can claim the difference as a capital gain and increase pretax profits by $50 million. Alternatively, the profit could be amortized over the life of the lease. Due to GAAP ambiguities and loopholes, firms can choose the methods that benefit them the most.

Both taking reserves for bad loans and the real estate sale/leaseback are perfectly legal. However, their accounting treatment assumes that these transactions occur as normal business activities, but some firms use them as accounting devices to manage earnings over time. Other firms can be used as examples for managing earnings. For instance, IBM has also been accused of taking financial steps in the 1990s to create double-digit earnings growth when revenue grew at only 5 percent.[3] However, GE holds a special place in the investment industry because it is the only company in the Dow Jones Industrial Average that was an original Dow Jones firm when the index was created more than 100 years ago.

The accounting schemes that companies use can be either simple or quite complex. Indeed, modern accounting and auditing firms recommend structuring deals in a way that may not have any value in conducting business, but the deals spin off either profits or losses that can be reversed in the future to manage earnings. A question often asked is how much can companies manipulate accounting figures before they cross the line into fraud? Where is the line?

For example, a firm could sell an asset, such as a truck, to its own subsidiary (for example, technically a special-purpose entity created as an off-shore partnership) for an outrageously high price. The book value of the truck is low. Therefore, the firm books a large capital gain and profits go up. The subsidiary capitalizes the cost of the truck, which means that the subsidiary will have to report lower earnings in each of the future years in which the truck cost is depreciated. In effect, the firm takes a profit now that it will have to offset as expenses in the future related to the sale of a truck it still owns! While these types of maneuvers help to manage earnings, their effect is limited unless the company crosses the line and uses them fraudulently.

The pressure on accounting departments to smooth earnings, or even produce earnings, can be intense when the firm is not meeting investor (and analyst) expectations. Because the role of accounting has changed and accounting departments are viewed as profit centers, they are pressed to make up shortfalls created by the business operations of the firm. Sometimes, firms stoop to fraudulent practices.

BOX 3-2

EXAMPLE–RITE AID CORPORATION

On June 21, 2002, a federal grand jury indicted four former and current executives of Rite Aid for conducting a wide-ranging scheme to overstate income.[4] The SEC noted in its investigation of the matter that Rite Aid reported false and misleading information in 10 different areas ranging from reducing its costs and accelerating revenue to manipulating numbers between quarterly and annual reports.[5] Indeed, Rite Aid restated earnings for its fiscal year 1998 in a way that caused $305 million in net income to become $186 million in net losses. The restatement in fiscal year 1999 was from a $143 million profit to a $422.5 million loss, and a total of more than $1 billion in earnings disappeared.

Figure 3.2 shows the price of Rite Aid's stock during this period and its relationship to stated and restated earnings. Rite Aid stated that it earned $116.7 million in fiscal year 1997, which ended February 28, 1998. The stock price at this time was $21 per share. As indicated above, Rite Aid then stated earnings of $305 million in 1998, and the stock price rose to $34.25. The stock price reached its maximum of $50.94 on January 8, 1999. A few months later the firm reported fiscal year 1999 earnings of $143 million. However, investors started to realize that something was wrong. By July 10, 2000, the stock had slowly fallen to $7.85 per share. The stock price fell to $5 per share the next day when Rite Aid restated its earnings for 1998 to 2000. The stock spent the summer of 2002 at less than $2.50 per share.

FIGURE 3.2   RITE AID EARNINGS AND ASSOCIATED STOCK PRICE

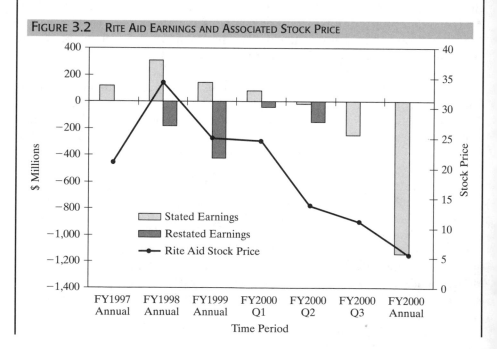

Rite Aid's stock price was artificially inflated in the late 1990s because of fraud in financial reporting. The investors who purchased Rite Aid stock in 1999 did so based on false information, thinking the firm profitable and growing. As a result they lost money. Existing investors should also have been informed about the extent of the firm's losses so that they could decide whether to keep or sell their stock. After the truth finally became public, it was too late—shareholders had lost most of their investments.

CONSULTANTS

Business consulting firms typically advise firms on tactical issues, such as how to enter a new market, and strategic issues, such as acquiring or spinning off other firms. When it comes to consulting, the leading firm is McKinsey & Company, which advises more than half of the Fortune 500 firms. In 2001, McKinsey had 7,700 consultants in 84 locations worldwide and generated $3.4 billion in revenue.[6] This represents a more than 40 percent market share of the consulting business. Accounting firms want to gain some of this business.

One potential problem for a firm's shareholders occurs when a consulting firm also conducts auditing services for the company. The income for conducting an audit is far lower than the fees earned for consulting. Therefore, auditors may be pressured by their own accounting firm to overlook borderline practices, especially when consultants advocate those practices. This situation represents a serious conflict of interest for the auditors. Their responsibility should be effective monitoring for the shareholders, but instead their inclination may be different because their bonuses often depend on how much money the consulting group earns for the accounting firm.

The Public Company Accounting Reform and Investor Protection Act of 2002, which is intended to separate auditors and consultants, prohibits accounting firms from providing both auditing and consulting activities to the same company. This law will reduce the conflict of interest faced by auditors, and it might actually create conflict between the firm's consultants and its auditors. However, this law does not affect the long-standing relationship between auditors and their client firms. Whether the new law will encourage auditors to challenge a firm and whether auditors will discourage dubious accounting strategies is still unclear.

BOX 3-3

EXAMPLE–TYCO INTERNATIONAL LTD.

Consultants commonly advise companies on tax reduction strategies. Consider the efforts that Tyco International Ltd. makes to reduce its U.S. taxes. Tyco, an electrical manufacturing and services firm, moved to the tax haven of Bermuda in 1996.[7] The company has also created more than 150 subsidiaries in other tax-friendly places like Barbados and the Cayman Islands. The purpose of these entities is not, for the most part, to conduct business, but to shelter income from the United States and to avoid taxes. Tyco claims that these strategies cut its 2001 tax bill by $600 million, and Tyco pays the most taxes to countries other than the United States. All this happens beyond the eyes of the shareholder. The annual report does not provide information about its mysterious subsidiaries, which have names like Driftwood, Bunga Bevaru, and Silver Avenue Holdings.

AN INTERNATIONAL PERSPECTIVE

Compared to the accounting systems used internationally, the system in the United States is quite rigorous. Characteristics of a high-quality system are many shareholder rights and strong protection of those rights. This protection comes from strong laws that are enforced and accounting standards that are unambiguous.

In a recent study of 31 countries, the United States was found to have the best legal environment to discourage earnings manipulations and smoothing.[8] Australia, Ireland, Canada, and the United Kingdom also have good investor protection and enforcement histories. Countries where earnings manipulations are more common include Austria, Italy, Germany, South Korea, and Taiwan. While some shareholders might question the quality of the financial statements in the United States, the accounting numbers of some firms that are not based in the United States could be of much lower quality. The scandals in some U.S. firms parallel some recent international scandals.

The International Accounting Standards Board (IASB) is developing a single set of high-quality, understandable, and enforceable global accounting standards that require transparent and comparable information in general-purpose financial statements. In addition, IASB wants to encourage convergence in accounting standards of individual countries around the world. Whether the SEC will accept financial statements using these international standards rather than U.S. GAAP remains to be seen.

❖ SUMMARY

The average shareholder who reads annual reports could not have predicted the corporate scandals of 2001 and 2002. The accounting issues are too well hidden in the financial statements and their treatment is too complex. Instead, shareholders rely on the governance system to interpret financial statements and comment on the financial health and prospects of the firm. While financial analysts and credit rating agencies (both to be discussed later) also provide interpretations, shareholders depend a great deal on auditors. After all, among outsiders, auditors are the most knowledgeable about the firm's business activities.

Auditors are an important part of the governance system. However, to be effective monitors, auditors must be credible, and they are most credible when they are independent of the company being audited and free from conflicts of interest. One conflict of interest, auditing and consulting, has been resolved. However, the difficulty still exists that auditing firms want to keep the public company as a client over the long term. This makes them less aggressive in routing out problems because management can easily threaten the firing of the auditing firm.

QUESTIONS

1. Smoothing earnings makes the time series of earnings less volatile. This could make the stock price less volatile (i.e., less risky). So, is smoothing, or managing, carnings good or bad for shareholders? Compare and contrast the advantages versus disadvantages of smoothing earnings.

2. Periodically, a firm might decide that its financial statements do not accurately reflect its financial condition.

When the firm provides new financial statements, it is said to have *restated*. The number of earnings restatements has dramatically changed over the past decade. How and why has the number changed?

3. What is the relationship between auditors and the SEC?

4. Name and describe the conflicts of interest auditors face.

EXERCISES

1. Accounting scandals have recently occurred in firms outside the United States. Find one of these firms and describe what the firm did and how it was discovered

2. What happened to the (now defunct) auditing firm, Arthur Andersen?

3. Enron continuously pushed the envelope with regard to its accounting practices. Find some examples of how Enron used legal accounting methods to fraudulently misrepresent its financial condition.

4. WorldCom disclosed that roughly $3.8 billion had been improperly booked as capital investments instead of operating expenses. Describe how this affected its financial statements, stock price, and credit rating.

ENDNOTES

1. There are limitations on how different public reporting and IRS reporting can be.

2. Jon Birger, "Glowing Numbers," *Money Magazine* (November 2000):112–122.

3. Spencer Ante and David Henry, "Can IBM Keep Earnings Hot?" *Business Week* (April 15, 2002):58–60.

4. Reuters, "SEC Charges Ex-Rite Aid Execs with Fraud" (June 21, 2002): 11:05 a.m.

5. Rite Aid Corporation, Accounting and Auditing Enforcement Release No. 1579, *Securities and Exchange Commission*, June 21, 2002.

6. John Byrne, "Inside McKinsey," *Business Week* (July 8, 2002):66–76.

7. William Symonds, "The Tax Games Tyco Played," *Business Week* (July 1, 2002):40–41.

8. Christian Leuz, Dhananjay Nanda, and Peter Wysocki, "Investor Protection and Earnings Management: An International Comparison," Wharton School working paper, May 2002.

THE BOARD OF DIRECTORS

What are the responsibilities of a board of directors? In general, a board of directors is charged with four broad functions: (1) to hire, evaluate, and perhaps even fire top management, with the position of CEO being the most important to consider; (2) to vote on major operating proposals (e.g., large capital expenditures and acquisitions); (3) to vote on major financial decisions (e.g., issuance of stocks and bonds, dividend payments, and stock repurchases); and (4) to offer expert advice to management. In executing these functions, directors are supposed to represent the interests of the shareholders.

A great deal of important board work occurs at the subcommittee level and subsequently goes to the full board for approval. Some boards include an executive committee, a finance committee, and a community relations committee, among others. The most common board subcommittees are the audit committee, the compensation committee, and the nomination committee.[1] The audit committee is charged with finding an independent auditor for the firm's accounting statements, and the committee must ensure that the auditor will do its job objectively. The compensation committee is responsible for designing the executive compensation package. The nomination committee searches for and nominates candidates to run for impending vacancies among board seats in annual shareholder elections. A separate stock options subcommittee has gained popularity with boards in recent years, probably due to the controversy surrounding stock options.

While the board's role in the corporation seems to ensure that shareholder interests are being considered, there are some potentially serious problems. Among the issues are a lack of board independence from the CEO, directors who do not have the time or expertise to fulfill their roles adequately, and members who do not have a vested interest in the firm. This chapter provides an overview of corporate boards and their role in corporate governance, and it also highlights potential problems with many of today's boards.

HISTORICAL PERSPECTIVE

In 1934, William O. Douglas, a law professor who later served as the SEC chairman for 36 years, claimed that directors do not direct. For the most part, his assertion has held true for quite some time. One director boasted in 1962, "If you have five directorships, it is total heaven, like having a permanent hot bath. No effort of any kind is called for. You go to a meeting once a month in a car supplied by the company, you look grave and sage, and on two occasions say, 'I agree.'"[2]

By all reports, conditions have changed dramatically for the better, but this is primarily a recent trend. During the past 15 years or so, shareholders have become increasingly more demanding of directors, and, as a result, directors have been working longer hours, taking more stock ownership in the firm to ensure a vested interest, challenging the CEO more often, and taking their duties more seriously. These demands are starting to take their toll on directors. According to recruiters Christian & Timbers, 60 percent of nominated directors are turning down appointments. Nonetheless, with director compensation averaging more than $40,000 per year—along with perks, travel, stocks, and stock options—all for working about 150 hours and attending eight meetings a year, directorship is lucrative.[3]

MORE ATTENTION ON DIRECTORS

Even before recent corporate meltdowns and scandals, the general public started to pay more attention to directors and their activities. Prior to the mid-1980s, the public paid little heed to directors and thought them merely ornamental features of corporations. However, the situation has changed. The demand for better corporate governance has occurred partly as a response to the tidal wave of mergers and acquisitions (M&A) activity of the 1980s. Figure 4.1 shows the deal value (in billions of dollars) of all acquisitions in the United States from 1968 to 1995.[4]

The figure shows that M&A activity increased dramatically during the 1980s. There are several reasons for this increase, including a more favorable tax environment, the increased popularity and availability of junk bonds to finance acquisitions, additional foreign competition, and deregulation in some industries. A recession and the collapse of the junk bond market resulted in a temporary M&A decline during the late 1980s, but M&A activity was strong again in the mid- and late-1990s.

Why would an increase in M&A activity lead to more board scrutiny? When one firm acquires another, it usually has to pay significantly more than the going market price. This situation is advantageous for the target firm's shareholders but

FIGURE 4.1   YEARLY VALUE OF MERGERS AND ACQUISITIONS

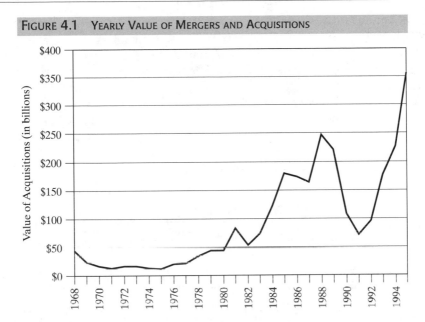

not for the acquiring firm's shareholders. Both boards must approve the acquisition before it goes to a shareholder vote. Consequently, the shareholders of both the potential acquirers and targets keep a close eye on their respective boards. For the acquirer, the shareholders may not wish to pay too much for a target, or may not wish to acquire the target at all. For the target firm, the shareholders may want to make sure that management does not adopt anti-takeover amendments, such as poison pills, that would make it difficult for the firm to be acquired for a nice price.

The corporate takeover market is an important disciplinary force for managers. If managers run a firm poorly, then it may be taken over by people who think they can run it more profitably. Shareholders want their firms to be profitable, so boards should ensure that anti-takeover amendments are not adopted. In summary, the takeover wave of the 1980s brought more attention to boards.

Boards of directors also received more scrutiny from shareholders because of two rules adopted by the SEC in 1992. First, the SEC required additional disclosure from corporations with regard to executive compensation, including the reporting of granted stock option values. When the values of these compensation contracts were disclosed, shareholders learned that CEOs were receiving millions of dollars per year in salary, bonuses, and stock options. In many cases, lavish compensation was granted even if the firm was not doing that well or was unprofitable. As such, shareholders began pressuring directors to make sure that the executives deserved what they were earning. The SEC also made it easier for shareholders to communicate with one another. Large institutional investors such as the pension funds California Public Employees' Retirement System

(CalPERS) and Teachers Insurance and Annuity Association—College Retirement Equities Fund (TIAA-CREF) took advantage of this rule. As a result, they were able to create stronger shareholder coalitions that in turn made it easier to put pressure on boards to challenge management. Institutional shareholder activism will be discussed in a later chapter.

The increased takeover market and the new regulatory environment caused shareholders and the general public to put more pressure on directors to do their jobs. However, because these changes occurred or took shape only recently, the avid attention being paid to boards is a recent phenomenon. For example, *Business Week* only started rating corporate boards in 1996.

BOARD REGULATIONS

No federal law explicitly dictates that public corporations must have a board of directors. Instead, corporations must follow the statute of the state in which they are incorporated. Some states have established lax corporate laws to encourage incorporation in the state and, therefore, more tax revenue. This situation explains why more than 300,000 firms are incorporated in Delaware. Fortunately, every state requires that a corporation have a board of directors.

The Model Business Corporation Act provides a guideline that states, "All corporate powers shall be exercised by or under authority of, and the business affairs of a corporation shall be managed under the direction of a board of directors."[5] Furthermore, "the fundamental *responsibility of the individual corporate director is to represent the interest of the shareholders as a group*, as the owners of the enterprise, in dealing with the business and affairs of the corporation with the law." (Italics added for emphasis.) As such, the board's fiduciary responsibility is clearly to the shareholders.

The stock exchanges NYSE (New York Stock Exchange) and Nasdaq—which, as self-regulatory organizations (SROs), can impose their own set of regulations—require that firms have an audit committee consisting primarily of independent directors. Since the scandals of 2001 and 2002, the exchanges have revised their regulations regarding the structure and function of a board of directors and the incentives provided to its members. Specifically, the NYSE mandates that companies have a *majority* of independent directors. A director is not independent if he or she (or immediate family) has worked for the company or its auditor within the past five years. Board members who are not also executives of the company *must meet regularly* without the presence of management. This move to increase the independence of boards is long overdue.

The NYSE also requires specific functions of the board. For example, the *nominating committee of the board must be composed entirely of independent directors* and must perform certain duties. The same holds true of the compensation committee. Otherwise, executives would have undue influence over their own compensation. The audit committee must also be independent, however, the members of this committee have an *increased authority and responsibility to hire and fire the auditing firm.* To handle this expanded responsibility, audit committee members must have the necessary experience and expertise in finance and accounting. To help maintain the independence of the audit committee, these board members may not receive compensation from the company, especially consulting fees, other than their regular director fees.

In the summer of 2002, the Sarbanes-Oxley Act, otherwise known as the Public Company Accounting Reform and Investor Protection Act of 2002, was passed. One section of the bill attempts to increase the monitoring ability and responsibilities of boards of directors and to improve their credibility. Specifically, the law makes the audit committee of the board of directors both more independent from management and more responsible for the hiring and oversight of auditing services and the accounting complaint process.

WHO ARE DIRECTORS?

Standard & Poor's 500 firms have about 11 directors each. How are these 5,500 or so board seats filled? The people nominated by the firm's management or board's nominating committee often become directors. According to the 2001 Korn/Ferry annual board of directors study, about two-thirds of directors say that the CEO or chairman has the most influence in identifying new directors. University deans or presidents and politicians are viewed as respectable figureheads, but most directors are executives of other firms. For example, Korn/Ferry states that a person would have to possess 10 to 20 years of experience in a business leadership role, be a current COO or CFO of a large company, or be one of the top 15 executives at a very large corporation to be considered a viable candidate for director. Sometimes a large individual shareholder submits a proposal to obtain a board seat. If the person is well-known or wealthy enough to launch an expensive campaign, he or she might gather enough votes to be elected.

According to the 2001 Korn/Ferry study, 91 percent of *Fortune*-listed firms have a retired executive serving as a director, 83 percent have an executive from another firm, 56 percent have an academic, and 52 percent have a former government official. With regard to gender and race representation, board diversity seems to be improving. Seventy-four percent of boards have a woman as a director, and 65 percent have a member of an ethnic minority, with African Americans sitting on 41 percent of our nation's boards.

PROBLEMS WITH BOARDS

One of the main functions of the board is to evaluate top management, especially the CEO. For many firms, however, the board's chairman is also the firm's CEO. Among the 30 firms that are included in the Dow Jones Industrial Average, which consists of the United States' major corporations, only eight firms have a separate CEO and board chair. For the *Fortune*-listed firms, only 10 percent have a non-executive chairman. Therefore, the same person who manages the firm also runs the board meetings and its agenda and is consequently the one who controls the information given to the board. This being the case, is the board capable of seriously evaluating or challenging the CEO? It can happen, but usually only as a result of significant shareholder pressure.

Even if the CEO is not the board chair, he or she is not necessarily under a more careful watch. While most boards have more outsiders than insiders (according to the Korn/Ferry study, the average board has three times as many outside directors as insider directors, where insiders are defined as a company employee), many of these so-called outside board members have some sort of business or personal tie to the CEO.

BOX 4-1

EXAMPLE–DISNEY'S BOARD

The Walt Disney Company CEO is Michael Eisner. As such, he is supposed to be monitored by Disney's board of directors. However, Disney's board has been criticized by *Business Week* as one of the worst in corporate America, and it has consisted of numerous current Disney managers, such as the chief corporate officer (CCO) and heads of various Disney operations. Disney claims, however, that 13 of the 16 board members are independent directors. These "outsiders" include Reveta Bowers, headmaster of the school that Eisner's children attended; George Mitchell, a paid consultant to Disney and an attorney whose law firm represents Disney; Stanley Gold, president of Shamrock Holdings, which manages investments for the Disney family; Leo O'Donovan, president of Georgetown University, which one of the Eisner children attended and which received donations from Eisner; Irwin Russell, Eisner's personal attorney; and Robert Stern, architect for several Disney projects.

Will Disney's board challenge Eisner? Not only do some of these directors work for Eisner, but there are obviously others who also benefit from not angering him. In other words, this board has too many insiders and those with business or other vested interests with the CEO. A lucrative contract penned for Eisner netted him more than $700 million in the last years of the 1990s. Disney's market value fell to less than half of what it was during the run-up of the 1990s. Even after this poor performance, Eisner is still firmly in control at Disney.

The boards of firms that have been reeling from scandal (for example, Tyco, Global Crossings, and Adelphia) were filled with former or current executives. Furthermore, one of Tyco's outside directors was paid $10 million for helping to arrange the acquisition of CIT Group. Former Adelphia CEO John Rigas, along with his three sons, held four out of the nine board seats. Can this quartet be expected to be objective monitors?

Another problem with some boards is that directors do not have a significant vested interest in the firm. For example, most of Disney's outside directors own little or no stock. In 1997, *Business Week* reported that the Occidental Petroleum board had approved a $95 million payout to its CEO, but two of its board members, George O. Nolley and Aziz D. Syriani, only owned 2,280 and 1,450 shares of the firm's stocks, respectively, despite the fact that they had sat on the board for 14 years.[6] The article also reported that Advanced Micro Devices director Charles M. Blalack and Microsoft director Richard Hackborn owned no shares of their firm. Can these board members empathize with their shareholders? Probably not.

However, the situation has been changing. For example, some firms, such as Ashland Inc., are setting stock ownership targets for their directors. To Eisner's credit, he has asked his directors to own more stock. For GE, the outside directors are clearly aligned with shareholders, as they own (at the beginning of the year 2000), an average of $6.6 million dollars of GE stock each.[7] According to the 2001 Korn/Ferry study, 53 percent of the directors were required to own some of the board's company stock.

In general, should we really worry about the lack of independence and lack of stock ownership of some directors? It is fairly well documented in academic studies that boards dismiss CEOs primarily if the stock price has been declining dramatically or if earnings have been significantly down. According to these same studies, those boards that fired a CEO were often ones that consisted of independent directors who held a large portion of firm's stock.[8] In other words, boards that were more objective and had more personal wealth at stake were more willing to make the dramatic decision to fire the CEO. When CEOs do get fired, some of the directors aligned with the CEO are also asked to resign, perhaps as a way of getting rid of the whole regime.[9] Therefore, directors can serve a meaningful monitoring role for the corporation, rather than a symbolic one, but there has to be enough of them who are independent from the CEO.

Are directors capable of providing the time and expertise required to understand fully and to approve the major operating and financial decisions of the firm? Some directors, especially those who are potentially good in that role, may be overextended. For example, many directors serve on multiple boards. According to a 1997 *Business Week* article, several people held directorships in ten or more firms.[10] Coca-Cola has five directors (out of 13) who serve on at least five boards. In addition, most directors also have their own highly demanding full-time jobs. Often, they are company executives themselves.

In addition, some directors simply do not have the expertise to be a board member. This means that independence, in and of itself, is not a sufficient quality for being an effective director. Some boards want to have a few figureheads, such as a celebrity (O.J. Simpson was once on the audit committee of Infinity Broadcasting) or a former army general, but other candidates probably could offer more. According to one academic study, having bank executives on boards, even those whose bank is not linked to the firm, turns out to be very useful because of credit market expertise.[11]

Finally, some boards are simply too big, which makes it more unlikely that all directors will be actively involved and more difficult to accomplish needed work. When there are many directors, any one may conveniently believe that others are doing the monitoring job, and they therefore may feel they do not have to work as hard. On a small board, each director knows that he or she must do more work because there are fewer to do it. Disney's board has 16 members, and Enron's had 15 members. Is this too big, and is this part of the problem? Academic researchers believe so. According to some studies, firms with fewer directors have higher market values, indicating their effectiveness.[12]

In summary, many potential problems plague boards today. Many directors might not be truly independent, they might be too busy, and they might not have the expertise to carry out their obligations. These problems seem to explain why some corporate scandals occur.

BOX 4-2

EXAMPLE—IS ENRON'S BOARD PARTIALLY TO BLAME?

Enron's board, which consisted of 15 members, epitomized the notion of one that is "captive" to the firm's CEO. Board member John Wakeham was a British Conservative Party politician who had approved the building of an Enron power plant in Britain in 1990. Four years later Wakeham was on the Enron board. Director Herbert Winokur is chairman and CEO of Capricorn Holdings. He also sat on the board of National Tank Company, which sold equipment and services to Enron divisions for millions of dollars. Directors Charles LeMaistre and John Mendelsohn were former president and president, respectively, of the M. D. Anderson Cancer Center, which received more than $500 million from Enron and its chairman, Ken Lay, during a five-year period. Director Wendy Gramm, a former chairwoman of the Commodity Futures Trading Commission, backed several policies that benefited Enron and other energy trading companies before she joined the Enron board. Her husband, Senator Phil Gramm, is a major recipient of Enron campaign donations. Board member Robert Belfer is founder and former chairman and CEO of Belco Oil and Gas Corporation. Belco and Enron had numerous financial arrangements. Director Charles Walker is a tax lobbyist. Firms partly owned by Walker were paid more than $70,000 by Enron for consulting services. In addition, Enron also made donations to a nonprofit corporation chaired by Walker. A Senate report argues that the board failed in their fiduciary duties to represent shareholders, and that the Enron failure was partly due to the lack of the board's independence.

In 1999, auditors had already told Enron board members that the company was using accounting practices that "push[ed] limits" and were "at the edge" of what was acceptable. One director, Robert Jaedicke, had been an accounting professor at Stanford University. Also, the board knowingly allowed Enron to move more than half of its assets off the balance sheet. Governance experts used by the Senate investigation stated that this activity was unheard of, but only one Enron board member expressed any concern when it was occurring. The board even waived a code of conduct stipulation for CFO Andrew Fastow, allowing him to create private offshore partnerships that would conduct business with Enron. Under the Enron code of conduct, no employee is allowed to obtain financial gain from an entity that does business with Enron. Under Fastow's watch, these entities profited at Enron's expense, but the board idly sat by despite Fastow's obvious conflict of interest.

The Senate report concludes that the board missed a dozen red flags that should have warned them about possible shenanigans at the firm. For example, directors were told that in a six-month period, Fastow's partnerships had generated $2 billion in funds for Enron. While Enron's board apparently was not involved in the fraud, they should have put a stop to it.[13] After all, they were being paid more than $350,000 a year in salary, stocks, and stock options by Enron to be its directors. In the Senate report's conclusion, they state, "much that was wrong with Enron was known to the Board.... By failing to provide sufficient oversight and restraint to stop management excess, the Enron Board contributed to the company's collapse and bears a share of the responsibility for it."[14]

❖ **SUMMARY**

A firm's board of directors plays a very important role in reducing problems inherent in the separation of ownership and control. Indeed, the board is responsible for hiring, evaluating, and sometimes firing the firm's executives. In addition, the board oversees the firm's auditors and makes major strategic decisions for the firm. They are to conduct these activities in the best interests of the shareholders.

Shareholders have only recently started paying attention to the activities of boards of directors. There are many potential problems with the organization of many corporate boards. For example, it seems that many directors lack the independence, the vested interest, the time, and sometimes the expertise to carry out their fiduciary obligations to shareholders. Enron's board is a telling example. However, the recent attention directed to boards has caused some changes to occur, but it is too early to tell if these changes are taking hold.

QUESTIONS

1. What are the primary roles of boards and board subcommittees?
2. How did the increased merger activity in the 1980s increase the attention given to corporate boards?
3. What regulations govern the functions and construction of boards of directors? What is required of boards?
4. What are the main problems in modern boards? How might they be changed to fix those problems?

EXERCISES

1. Examine the 30 firms in the Dow Jones Industrial Average. Which firms have the same person holding the CEO and board chairman titles?

2. Pick a company and identify all the board directors, their affiliation, and their compensation from the directorship. Much of this information can be obtained from proxy statements the firm files with the SEC.
3. Find three recent cases where the CEO of a firm was fired. What happened?
4. In the summer of 2002, WorldCom declared bankruptcy. It was the largest bankruptcy in history. Investigate what happened and how its board directors might have been complicit in the problems.

ENDNOTES

1. *28th Annual Board of Directors Study*, Korn/Ferry International, (Los Angeles, CA, 2001).
2. Katrina Brooker, "Trouble in the Boardroom," *Fortune* (May 13, 2002):113–116.
3. These statistics are based on averages reported in the *28th Annual Board of Directors Study*, Korn/Ferry International, 2001.
4. Source: *www.mergerstat.com*
5. Nasser Arshadi and Thomas H. Eyssell, *The Law and Finance of Corporate Insider Trading: Theory and Evidence* (Boston, MA: Kluwer Academic Publishers, 1993), p. 7.
6. "Directors in the Hot Seat," *Business Week* (December 8, 1997):100–104.
7. "The Best and Worst Corporate Boards," *Business Week* (January 24, 2000) from *www.businessweek.com*.
8. Jerold B. Warner, Ross L. Watts, and Karen H. Wruck, "Stock Prices and Top Management Changes," *Journal of Financial Economics* 20 (1989): 461–492; Michael S. Weisback, "Outside Directors and CEO Turnover," *Journal of Financial Economics* 20 (1988): 431–460; Kenneth A. Borokhovich, Robert Parrino, and Teresa Trapani, "Outside Directors and CEO Selection," *Journal of Financial and Quantitative Analysis* 31, no. 3 (1996): 337–355; Kathleen A. Farrell and David A. Whidbee, "The Consequences of Forced CEO Succession for Outside Directors," *The Journal of Business* 73, no. 4, (2000): 597–627.
9. Kathleen A. Farrell and David A. Whidbee, "The Consequences of Forced CEO Succession for Outside Directors," *Journal of Business* 73, no. 4 (2000): 597–627.
10. John A. Byrne, Leslie Brown, and Joyce Barnathan, "Directors in the Hot Seat," *Business Week* (December 8, 1997):100–104.
11. James R. Booth and Daniel N. Deli, "On Executives of Financial Institutions as Outside Directors," *Journal of Corporate Finance* 5, no. 3 (1999): 227–250.
12. Jeff Huther, "An Empirical Test of the Effect of Board Size on Firm Efficiency," *Economics Letters* 54, no. 3, (1996): 259–264; David Yermack, "Higher Market Valuation of Companies with a Small Board of Directors", *Journal of Financial Economics* 40, no. 2 (1996): 185–211.
13. John Byrne, "Commentary: No Excuses for Enron's Board," *Business Week* (July 29, 2002) from *www.businessweek.com*.
14. Source: "The Role of the Board of Directors in Enron's Collapse," U.S. Senate Report 107–170, July 8, 2002.

CHAPTER 5

INVESTMENT BANKS

Most people are familiar with commercial banks because of their role in everyday living. Many people have savings accounts and checking accounts with a commercial bank, and some might have even borrowed money from them. Investments banks, however, play a quite different role from commercial banks.

Investment banks primarily help companies raise capital by issuing securities. Company managers are experts in the business activities of their particular industry, and they know how to build, market, sell, and service their products. However, these managers do not possess expertise in obtaining the capital they may need to develop new products or expand operations. In addition, financial engineering over the past decade has created some very complicated securities. Which securities should a firm sell to obtain capital? Should the firm sell securities to public investors or to deep pocket private investors like state pension funds? Indeed, even the process of registering new securities with the SEC is complicated. Investment banks specialize in steering firms through this maze of questions and helping them obtain needed capital with the most appropriate security issue.

Investment banks are compensated through service fees they charge to companies for selling new securities. After the firm receives the capital and the investors receive their securities, the investment bank no longer is involved. That is, investment banks put together one set of deals and then they move on to another. Because investment banks must evaluate their client firms' needs and because they bring investment opportunities to the market, they form an important and integral part of the corporate governance system. This chapter, beginning with some historical perspective, provides an overview of investing banking activities, and it also describes their role in the recent collapse of investor confidence that has hurt U.S. and other markets.

SOME HISTORICAL PERSPECTIVE

Modern U.S. investment banks descend from the merchant bank. Merchant banks used their own capital to stake goods traders in various risky endeavors, particularly in foreign trade in the 1600s and 1700s. In those days, conducting trade over long distances meant taking the risk of losing cargo to both weather and piracy as well as the normal risk of business, such as competition and product substitutes. Merchant banks helped to fund trade expeditions in exchange for a stake in the profits.

Merchant banks were especially active in the United States when they were still the British Colonies. Trade ships brought natural resources from America to Europe and returned with goods supplied from all over the world. These voyages were funded through merchant banks. After the Revolutionary War, a fledgling United States found that it had an abundance of natural resources and capitalistic spirit, but very little capital. Merchant banks set up private banks in the United States to help businesses obtain capital. These banks had contacts in Europe, the source of most capital at that time, and they became intermediaries between the sources of capital and American businesses.[1] Junius Spencer Morgan founded one of the best-known firms, J.S. Morgan and Company. Junius, along with his son and grandson, were particularly adept at funneling foreign capital to the United States. His son, John Pierpont Morgan, ran the activities in America and eventually named that operation J.P. Morgan. Today, the firm is called J.P. Morgan Chase & Company. Of course, much has changed since the post-colonial days. Now the United States is the greatest source of capital in the world. Foreign firms and even foreign countries issue securities in the United States to obtain capital.

In the early 1800s, most investment banking activities consisted of treasury, municipal, and railroad bonds. These early investment banks also helped to set up new markets in the United States. For example, Marcus Goldman established Goldman Sachs and Company in 1869 and created the U.S. commercial paper market. Commercial paper is a security similar to U.S. Treasury Bills except that financially strong companies issue them, not the government.

The differences between commercial bank and investment bank activities began to vanish in the mid-1920s. The excesses of the 1920s were similar to that of the late 1990s. The economy was strong and the stock market continuously advanced. The government inadvertently contributed to the exuberance in 1927 by allowing commercial banks to participate in the stock issuance process. From 1926 to 1928, the number of new stock issues increased eight-fold, and many new companies came to the market.

As described later in this chapter, different methods exist for a bank to help issue stock. One process is called *underwriting*, which involves the bank taking some risk. The bank guarantees that the company issuing the security will receive a specific amount of capital. If the stock does not sell, the bank loses money. This situation had a large impact on commercial banks in the stock market crash of 1929. Banks were stuck with stock they could not sell, and in turn, the losses of the banks impacted depositors. Indeed, worried people with bank deposits demanded their money back. The panicky rush to the banks forced them to close and caused runs on other banks. Soon, the whole banking system was in a shambles, which contributed to the severity and duration of the Great Depression that followed.

After the stock market crash of 1929 and the following economic slowdown, the U.S. Congress held hearings and conducted investigations. Investors demanded reform. In the spring of 1933, a bill known as the Glass-Steagall Act of 1933 was introduced and passed relatively quickly. The law had two main components. The first was to create deposit insurance in order to regain the people's confidence in the banking system and faith in the safety of commercial banks. The second part was separation of commercial banking and investment banking. Investment banks could not receive deposits from the public and commercial banks could not conduct underwriting activities.

History tends to repeat itself. By the early 1980s, U.S. commercial banks were lobbying Congress to allow them into investment banking activities. The Federal Reserve Board finally allowed commercial banks to underwrite commercial paper, municipal bonds, and asset backed securities (such as mortgage-backed bonds).[2] This decision went to the U.S. Supreme Court in 1988, which let it stand. At the same time, investment banks were moving into areas of commercial banking. For example, the money market mutual fund plays a similar role to a bank deposit. Much of the Glass-Steagall Act of 1933 was torn away in the Financial Services Modernization Act of 1999 (also known as the Gramm-Leach-Bliley Act), which allowed investment banks and commercial banks to affiliate with each other under one holding company structure. Several banks quickly merged into this structure. For example, J.P. Morgan Chase & Company is the financial holding company for two main banking entities, JPMorgan and Chase Manhattan Bank USA. JPMorgan is an investment bank while Chase Manhattan is a commercial bank.

Notice that investment banking and commercial banking merged in both 1927 and in 1999. Both cases occurred during the run-up of a stock market bubble and preceded a severe market decline.

INVESTMENT BANKING ACTIVITIES

The basic investment banking service is to help companies issue new debt and equity securities. A firm can issue several different kinds of securities. The bank advises the company on the optimal security for the amount of capital being raised, while taking into account the company's situation. For this service, investment banks charge the company a fee. The size of the fee depends on how much risk the investment bank takes to issue the securities. There are two methods that banks can use to issue stock and bonds: underwriting and best efforts.

Think about the case of issuing stock. When underwriting an issue, the bank will guarantee that the company will receive a specific amount of capital. That is, the banker assures the company that a certain number of shares will sell at a target price. If too few shares sell at that price, the investment bank must buy those shares. To illustrate the risk that the bank takes, consider what would have happened if an issue were being sold when the September 11, 2001, terrorist attacks occurred. Stock prices plummeted and investors were not interested in buying stock. If the bank guaranteed the company would gain $100 million in capital, and only $70 million was raised, the bank would have to buy $30 million worth of stock. The fee for underwriting a $100 million issue is typically about $7 million for a new issue (i.e., for an initial public offering, or IPO) and $5 million for issues raised by already existing public companies (i.e., for a seasoned equity offering, or SEO).

If the investment bank did not want to assume the risk on a security issue, it could use the best-efforts method. Here, there is no guarantee of raising the desired amount of capital. The banker does his or her best to sell as much of the security as possible for the company. In this case, the company takes the risk of not receiving enough capital. Because the risk is low for the investment bank, the fee charged is much lower for the best-efforts method than for underwriting.

The process of selling securities to public investors involves registration at the SEC. The document submitted to the SEC includes a preliminary prospectus containing information about the security issue and the company. For example, the prospectus details the company's financial condition, business activities, management experience, and how the funds raised will be used. The bank distributes the final prospectus to investors interested in the securities issue. Note that this information helps investors make decisions about the condition of the company and about buying the issue. In other words, investment bankers are another source of information and monitoring of a public company.

The prospectus and the banker's "road show" relay information about the company to investors. The road show is the marketing campaign done by bankers to pre-sell the issue. They travel the country visiting large institutional investors such as public pension funds and mutual funds. To sell to individual investors, investment banks use their brokerage operations. For a hot issue, investors call the brokers to order shares. In a less popular issue, the brokers call investors.

Information about the issuing company is especially important to investors when the firm is new. When a firm offers stock to the public for the very first time in an IPO, the company is typically young, small, and mostly unknown to investors. The information gathered by the investment bank and presented to the SEC may be the only independent data available on the firm. Therefore, investors expect the bank to disclose all relevant information in order to make good investment decisions.

Investment banks experience increased risk when underwriting an IPO because of the uncertainty involved with new firms. To mitigate some of the risk, banks tend to underprice IPO offerings. That is, banks offer the new shares of stock at a lower price than the demand for the stock would suggest. For example, on July 25, 2002, the newly public firm LeapFrog Enterprises conducted an IPO to raise $130 million. The company produces technology-enhanced toys and is considered a business of Michael Milken, the junk bond king of the 1980s. A syndicate of banks conducted the underwriting services for this deal, and those investors who purchased the stock from the syndicate bought it at $13 per share. However, there were not enough shares for all the investors who wanted them, and the investors who were left out of the deal had to buy shares on the New York Stock Exchange later that day. LeapFrog's stock price opened on the exchange at $15.50 per share and closed the day at $15.85. The first-day return for the stock was 22 percent. The investment banks were probably well aware that the first-day trading price would be greater than $13 per share, but they underpriced the stock offer anyway to ensure that they would sell all of the stock and reduce their liability to LeapFrog.

Underpricing IPOs lowers the risk to the underwriters and makes the new issues highly desirable to investors. After all, who would not want a 22 percent return in one day? Figure 5.1 shows the number of IPOs offered in each year from 1980 to 2001.[3] The line represents the average first-day return for the offerings each year. Note that the average first-day return is positive in every year, but that does not mean that every IPO experiences a price increase on the first day. Some IPOs are in high demand and earn a positive return—others are in low demand and decline in price the first day. Investors want the desirable IPO firms, not the lemons. The average initial return for IPOs in the late 1990s and 2000 was extraordinarily high. The average in 1999 was more than 70 percent! During the

FIGURE 5.1   IPOs ISSUED AND THEIR AVERAGE INITIAL RETURN FROM 1980 TO 2001

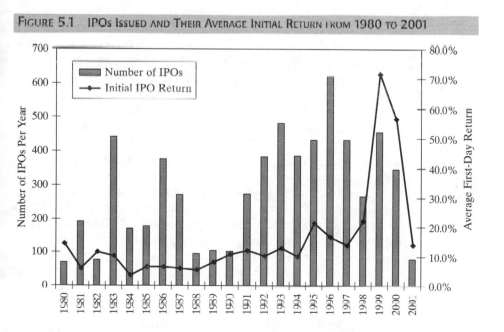

1990s, the average underpricing in the United States was just over 20 percent. This compares to 16.5 percent in France, 40.2 percent in Germany, and 39.6 percent in the United Kingdom.[4]

The number of IPOs offered correlates with a bull market. Stocks were in a strong bull market in the mid-1980s until the crash of October 1987. After the crash, the number of IPOs declined to approximately 100 per year. This number increased dramatically in the bull market of the 1990s. Then, after the bear market arrived in 2000, the number of IPOs again declined for 2001. The first six months of 2002 saw only 46 IPOs. In July 2002, during the lows of investor confidence, there were only five IPOs.

INVESTMENT BANK CRITICISMS

IPO PROBLEMS

Investment banks take small, private firms public in IPOs. These small firms want the capital that the stock issue provides to expand. Every small business owner would like to gain tens or hundreds of millions of dollars to spend, but very few small businesses would make good public companies. That is, the business model of many small firms would not work effectively as large, national firms. In addition, small business owners may not be capable of running a large business.

Typically only a small fraction (less than one percent) of firms that want to conduct an IPO actually do. Who decides which firms go public? Investment banks make this decision. After all, they take the risk as the underwriters. The banks thoroughly examine potential IPO firms. Traditionally, the policy of many banks has been to bring a firm public only if it has put together a good management team, developed a quality business plan, and perfected its business model enough so that it has earned profits in the past three quarters. The companies brought public from 1986 to 1995 experienced only a 1 percent failure rate.[5] This rate is defined as the firm's stock price falling to less than $1 (or delisted from the exchanges) within the first three years after the IPO. Investment banks did a good job of offering quality companies to investors during the late 1980s to the mid 1990s.

The situation began to change in the mid- to late-1990s. The stock prices of technology firms dramatically increased and were enormously popular with investors. The demand from investors for more technology stocks seemed insatiable. Hundreds of million of dollars were to be made by taking tech firms public. The investment banking industry raked in more than $2 billion in banking fees. There were not enough new firms that met the traditionally high quality standards of the banks, but investors did not seem to care. They seemed to want any new tech stock at any price. Notice how high the average first day returns of IPOs were in 1999 and 2000. The risk of underwriting these firms did not seem very high with such strong demand. To meet the high demand, banks began to bring inferior companies to the market.

BOX 5-1

EXAMPLE–PETS.COM

Consider the IPO of Pets.com. In 1999, the firm had only $5.8 million in revenue and reported an operating loss of $61.8 million. Yet Merrill Lynch launched the Pets.com IPO in February 2000. The firm raised $66 million in capital and Merrill received more than $4 million in fees.[6] Ten months later, Pets.com filed for bankruptcy and folded.

The firms that offered IPOs in the period 1998 to 2000 experienced a 12 percent failure rate, which is much higher than the historic 1 percent rate. Investment banks apparently lost their desire to be gatekeepers of quality firms and monitors for investors. Investors probably measure success differently; they measure it by their investment return. Of the 367 Internet firms that have gone public since 1997, only 15 percent have made money compared to their offer prices. More than 200 firms have lost more than 75 percent of their value. What made this even worse for individual investors is that the average investor rarely can access good IPOs at the offer price. Instead, such investors usually cannot buy the stock until it starts trading on the stock exchange. By then, the stock has typically already increased in price. Consequently, poor returns are even worse for the average individual investor.

STRUCTURED DEALS

When companies need more capital, or even just more cash, they turn to investment banks, which can be difficult. As an extreme example, consider a firm facing bankruptcy. In bankruptcy, the equity of the firm is taken from the stockholders, who gain nothing, and given to some of the creditors. Therefore, investors are not likely to buy additional shares of a financially troubled firm. The firm would also have trouble borrowing money from banks or from bond investors because these creditors typically do not recoup all their money. Banks or bond investors often receive only a small fraction of what they are owed and then are given some stock to become the new owners of the firm. Lenders do not get their money back in bankruptcy court, therefore they are unlikely to lend money to a financially troubled firm.

Often a firm has trouble raising capital even if it is not on the brink of bankruptcy. For example, the current creditors of the firm may have stipulated in their loans that the firm cannot borrow more money unless they are repaid first. Also, very few firms can successfully issue additional stock when investor confidence is low, as it was in the summer of 2002.

One criticism of investment banks is that they sometimes have been active participants in helping companies raise capital outside traditional avenues, thus manipulating earnings. Enron's strategy was to launch structured deals using special purpose entities (SPEs) created in tax havens such as the Cayman

Islands. The SPEs were formed as partnerships that created the appearance of third-party companies doing business with Enron. The "business" actually turned out to be loans that were not recorded as debt, but instead, recorded as revenue. For the structured deals to work, Enron needed complicated structures to fool auditors and regulators. To help create and fund the deals, Enron turned to investment banks. Large institutional investors frequently funded these partnerships.

BOX 5-2

EXAMPLE–ENRON'S PARTNERSHIPS

Enron invested heavily in an Internet start-up called Rhythms NetConnections. Rhythms stock had jumped, and the investment of $10 million grew to $300 million, a $290 million profit! Due to restrictions on selling ownership in the recent IPO, Enron could not sell this stock. Because of its mark-to-market method of accounting, Enron could book the gain. However, Enron worried that a big decline in price later would require booking a large loss.[7] Enron could not persuade the investment banks to hedge the price risk because of Enron's huge position in the high-risk start-up. Consequently, Enron created a partnership called LJM in the Cayman Islands that would guarantee the profit.[8] Enron CFO Andrew Fastow would run the partnership. The new partnership was funded by Enron stock. Therefore, Enron was really insuring itself. This profit would represent 30 percent of Enron's total profit for the year. The danger was that if both Rhythms stock and the Enron stock price fell, LJM would not have enough capital to make the guaranteed payment. Enron would then have to reverse the profit and record a loss of $290 million. The large loss would further depress the Enron stock. Even with this risk, Enron created LJM and completed the deal. Enron considered LJM a big success and entered into similar arrangements to hedge other risky tech stock holdings. They called these arrangements Raptor partnerships.

The myriad of partnerships created was actually a sophisticated Ponzi scheme. Enron dealt with nearly 700 SPEs in all. Enron created fictitious profits to meet earnings expectations. Those profits would have to be offset in the future as losses. As the losses came due, Enron continued the process and created new structured deals to hide (or delay) the losses and generate additional profits. In this way, the deals quickly mushroomed in number and in size. Eventually, the scheme collapsed when Enron's stock price fell in 2001. Many of the partnerships funded with the stock were unable to complete their transactions. Enron was forced to disclose $1 billion in losses that it had previously booked as profits and was forced into bankruptcy.

Investment banks have denied any wrongdoing, saying they are not responsible for Enron (or any other firm) fraudulently booking loans as revenue. However, the bankers had to know that Enron's financial statements were misleading—at the very least. Even if the banks did nothing illegal, they violated the trust of its clients and public investors by participating in a scheme designed to hide a firm's financial troubles. The institutions failed in their corporate governance role as a monitor. This failure is particularly concerning because Morgan and Citigroup (the two biggest players in the Enron fiasco) are the nation's two largest financial institutions.

While the Enron example details the role of investment banks in Enron's structured deals, evidence exists that banks have helped other firms create questionable SPEs. JP Morgan pitched these financing vehicles to other firms and entered into arrangements with seven companies. Citigroup discussed structured deals with 14 companies and developed them with three.[9] Deals have also been structured by the bankers of Credit Suisse Group, Barclays PLC, FleetBoston Financial Corporation, Royal Bank of Scotland Group PLC, and Toronto-Dominion Bank.

❖ SUMMARY

Investment banks play a vital role in the American corporate system: They help firms acquire the capital they need to expand business operations. This expansion contributes to the growth in economic activity, wealth, and job creation in a capitalist economy. In order to underwrite the securities firms' issue, the banks become intimately familiar with the operations of those firms. This situation gives them a unique ability to be corporate governance monitors. Capital is a scarce commodity, and investment banks must be the gatekeepers and ensure that deserving companies obtain needed capital. However, these institutions must conduct due diligence activities and bring only high quality firms and security issues to the public. Sometimes, the banks fail in this role.

QUESTIONS

1. What is the main role of investment banks in a capitalist economy? Describe how they fulfill that role.
2. Discuss why and how investment banks can effectively monitor corporations.
3. What are the main ways an investment bank offers a security for sale?
4. Why does it seem like IPOs are underpriced in the offering?

EXERCISES

1. The SEC believed that JP Morgan and Citigroup behaved unethically and illegally with regard to Enron. What have been the banks' consequences for this behavior?
2. Find a firm that recently conducted an IPO. What are the details of the offering? Which investment bank(s) underwrote the offering? How successful was the offering from the perspectives of the firm, the banks, and investors? Do you think the firm was ready to conduct an IPO?
3. Find a firm that is scheduled to conduct an IPO in the very near future. What types of information are provided to the interested investor? Is the information useful in making a buy decision?

4. Investment banks have argued that their financial engineering and structured deals can provide capital to firms that would have trouble raising capital in traditional ways. On the other hand, an inability to raise capital is a sign that the firm does not deserve capital, which is a scarce resource. Compare and contrast these two ideas.

ENDNOTES

1. This history is adapted from Charles Geisst, *Wall Street* (New York, NY: Oxford University Press, 1997).
2. David S. Kidwell, Richard Peterson, David W. Blackwell, and David A. Whidbee, *Financial Institutions, Markets, and Money*, 8th Edition (Hoboken, NJ: John Wiley and Sons, 2003).
3. Jay Ritter and Ivo Welch, "A Review of IPO Activity, Pricing, and Allocations," *Journal of Finance* 57, no. 4 (2002):1795–1828.
4. Alexander Ljungqvist and William Wilhelm, "IPO Allocations: Discriminatory or Discretionary?" *Journal of Financial Economics* 65, no. 2 (2002):167–201
5. Andrew Ross Sorkin, "Just Who Brought Those Duds to Market?" *New York Times*, April 15, 2001, 3.1.
6. Peter Elstrom, "The Great Internet Money Game," *Business Week* (April 26, 2001):16.
7. Peter Fusaro and Ross Miller, *What Went Wrong at Enron* (Hoboken, NJ: John Wiley and Sons, 2002).
8. Peter Behr and April Witt, "Visionary's Dream Led to Risky Business," *Washington Post*, July 28, 2002, A1.
9. Jathon Sapsford and Paul Beckett, "Citigroup, J.P. Morgan Marketed Enron-Type Deals to Other Firms," *Wall Street Journal*, July 23, 2002, C13.

CHAPTER 6

FINANCIAL ANALYSTS

This chapter discusses financial analysts, who investigate public firms, evaluate their performance, and assess their future prospects. Analysts frequently possess better information than most investors about a company and can probably make more precise earnings estimates than anyone else. Therefore, these professionals are in a good position to monitor the firm and identify problems for the shareholders.

Analysts generally fall into two types: buy-side and sell-side. Institutional investors, such as pension funds and mutual funds, hire analysts. Their purpose is to help decide which stocks the fund should buy; therefore, they are referred to as *buy-side analysts*. The recommendations of these analysts are not public, and they are only seen and used within the institution. Since few shareholders see their evaluations, these analysts do not contribute as much to the corporate monitoring system. Alternatively, brokerage and investment banks also employ analysts. These analysts hope that their research will generate enough interest in a security that their firm will generate trading commissions or underwriting business. As such, brokerage and investment bank analysts are commonly known as *sell-side analysts*, and they often appear to act like salespeople for the stocks that they cover. The recommendations of sell-side analysts are frequently made public. Many investors rely on these recommendations and therefore, analysts are a part of the corporate monitoring system.

In this chapter, we first consider traditional analyst roles in capital markets, which include conducting research and recommending securities to clients. An overall look at the quality of their recommendations follows. The chapter also explores how analysts are compensated, which is important to understanding the major conflict of interests that analysts face.

THE TRADITIONAL ROLE OF THE ANALYST

An analyst is supposed to analyze. To make a useful assessment of the firms they evaluate, analysts look at operating and financial conditions, immediate and long-term future prospects, the effectiveness of management teams, and the general industry outlook. Most analysts follow a specific industry to gain expertise in a particular sector. Based on their evaluations, analysts will make earnings predictions. Usually, they will try to predict the quarterly earnings per share (EPS) numbers. These predictions are useful to investors who rely on these estimates to determine the health of the companies in which they may or may not own stock. For example, many investors use P/E ratios (the market price of a share of stock divided by its annual earnings per share) as an important gauge of a stock's attractiveness as an investment. Some investors like to examine forward-looking P/E ratios. That is, they use a P/E ratio for next year's estimated earnings. Therefore, these earnings estimates are important and useful to investors.

Perhaps more important, the analyst also makes trading recommendations to investors. For example, an analyst may suggest buying or selling a particular stock. These recommendations usually boil down to one-word or two-word recommendations such as "accumulate" or "buy." Unfortunately, these one-word recommendations are not standardized in the brokerage industry, which may lead to some confusion. Table 6.1 illustrates this point.

Table 6.1 shows the stock rating system used by three different analysts' firms. A quick glance at the table reveals some potential problems. One analyst may use a five-category scale while another may use a four-category scale. Further, while analysts A and C both use a five-category scale, analyst A has two categories below average, while analyst C has only one below average. Also note that a buy recommendation from analyst A is his highest recommendation, but for analyst B, it is her second highest rating. Lastly, each firm's definition of a market outperformer may be different. Are the recommendations for the upcoming one- or two-year period? Is 5 percent or 10 percent considered outperformance? It all depends on the analyst's firm.

TABLE 6.1 THREE EXAMPLES OF ANALYST RECOMMENDATIONS

A	B	C
Buy	Strong Buy	Recommended List
Outperform	Buy	Trading Buy
Neutral	Hold	Market Outperformer
Underperform	Sell	Market Perform
Avoid		Market Underperformer

Given the recent scrutiny of analyst recommendations, there has been a trend toward making analysts' ratings less complicated. For example, analysts at Goldman Sachs, Lehman Brothers, Merrill Lynch, Morgan Stanley, and Prudential are now using a three-tier rating system to eliminate the ambiguity between ratings such as strong buy versus buy.[1]

Analyst recommendations should be timely. For example, if on a particular day an interested investor finds that the analyst's recommendation for a given stock is a buy, then that recommendation should reflect the analyst's most recent opinion. This means the recommendation should be updated frequently. If a news item breaks that could potentially affect an analyst's recommendation, then a revised and updated recommendation should be disseminated immediately. For his or her largest customers, the analyst may even make a phone call. However, a recommendation revision may sometimes have to go through an approval process, which may take a couple of days. Lengthy research reports that are mailed out or personally presented to potential investors may be a bit less than timely as well. Nonetheless, investors generally rely on analysts for *timely* advice.

The traditional role of the analysts is to conduct thorough analyses of their assigned firms to make earnings estimates and trading recommendations. Further, they should also make timely stock recommendations. Are analysts good at these functions?

QUALITY OF RECOMMENDATIONS

With regard to predicting earnings, analysts have consistently been slightly conservative. That is, analysts make earnings predictions that end up being slightly lower than the eventual actual earnings. This result may seem odd, especially given their known penchant for being overly optimistic. These "conservative" earnings predictions are well-known phenomena and involve two factors. First, companies like to meet or beat earnings expectations. Management will then be viewed as being good at their jobs, and the company will be viewed as being as good as, or better than, expected. Second, for analysts to do a good job predicting earnings, they need information. If analysts have full access to the firms that they follow, such as personal meetings with the CEO or other top executives, then their task becomes easier. Will a CEO be 100 percent cooperative with an analyst who sets the estimate too high? Probably not. In fact, Bill Gates and sales chief Steve Ballmer of Microsoft once purposely criticized *their own firm* to a bunch of analysts in order to depress their expectations. Later, on being told by one analyst that they had succeeded in painting a grim picture, Gates and Ballmer gave each other a high-five![2] This being the case, what is the general outcome of these two factors? Analysts make slightly conservative estimates because this is what management wants.[3] This result makes the CEO happy and willing to grant future access to the analyst. The analyst ends up being "off" on an estimate only by a very small margin and is still considered a good analyst.

The company will either make or beat the estimate, and it will be considered a good company. "Under promise, over deliver" is the name of this game.

The ability of analysts to predict earnings accurately may suffer in the future. Since October 2000, the SEC has prevented firms from divulging privileged information to any analyst. Information that the firm wishes to convey to an analyst must simultaneously be conveyed to the public. The SEC believes it unfair that some investors, through analysts, can learn private information that other investors cannot. The SEC policy creates a level playing field for all investors. For the analyst without privileged access to information, forecasting accuracy is likely to decline. However, forecasts now may possibly become more honest assessments of future earnings. The effect that this SEC regulation will have on analysts' forecasts cannot be predicted, but one academic study finds that, since the SEC regulation passed, forecasts have become less accurate.[4]

What about analysts' ability to recommend stocks? It is unclear whether analysts are any good at picking stocks. Older academic studies from the 1970s contended that analysts did *not* have good stock-picking abilities. However, more recent studies suggest that analysts may have some marginal ability as stock pickers.[5] If you were to buy stocks recommended as a "strong buy" during 1985 to 1996 and hold them until the rating was downgraded, you would have outperformed the market by 4.3 percent per year, not considering transactions costs. Analysts did indeed pick good stocks! If transaction costs were considered, you would have under performed the market by 3.6 percent. While the picks were good, they were not good enough to implement a successful trading strategy.

Perhaps even more revealing is the fact that during the first part of 2002, only 2 percent of all stocks carried a sell recommendation,[6] despite the unambiguous bearishness of the markets. Knowledgeable investors, however, know that a neutral or hold recommendation is really a sell signal. Nonetheless, the optimistic phrases used by analysts still promote a bullish attitude, and not all investors are knowledgeable.

ANALYST COMPENSATION

Sell-side analysts try to help their brokerage firms or banks gain trading commissions in the securities that they cover. That is, analysts hope that their research will generate enough interest in a security to spur an investor to trade in it.

However, investors are not even obligated to trade in securities with the firm from which they obtained information. Large investors, especially, will simply search for the best execution prices, regardless of the recommendation source. Shopping for best execution prices results from the elimination of fixed commission fees in 1975, when every brokerage firm made large commissions without having to compete in price. Without knowing how much an analyst really contributed to commission revenue, how are analysts compensated fairly for what they do? Quantifying analysts' contribution to their firms' profits is difficult.

Given the difficulties associated with merit-based compensation for analysts, a significant portion of analyst compensation is now based on reputation. For example, money managers and institutions participate in annual surveys, such as those conducted by *Institutional Investor*, where they rate and evaluate analysts along various dimensions. For each industry, analysts are ranked. A high ranking implies that the analyst is highly visible and is winning over customers. As such, they are likely to be compensated well. However, this form of evaluation may encourage analysts to spend more time promoting themselves rather than working on their analyses.

BOX 6-1

EXAMPLE–HOW MUCH DO ANALYSTS MAKE?

The answer is complicated because it depends on the firm. Senior analysts working for companies with no investment banking services earn an average of $500,000 per year. The average rises to $1.5 million per year for analysts employed by investment banks.[7] The top few analysts in the industry have earned closer to $10 or $20 million, depending on the particular year. Even relative rookies in the field often earn more than $100,000. Jack Grubman earned about $20 million per year. Grubman left Salomon Smith Barney in August 2002 while he and the firm were under investigation by regulators, and his severance package included $12 million in Citigroup stock and forgiveness of a $19 million loan.

A part of analysts' compensation has increasingly been dependent on the investment banking business that they can bring to the institution. For example, some star analysts have been receiving 75 percent of their compensation from the investment-banking side of the firm. As such, equity research departments seem more like a support function for investment banking. This trend bucks the traditional view of what analysts do for a living. This partnership between traditionally separate arms of an investing banking firm leads to a very serious conflict of interest problem.

POTENTIAL CONFLICTS OF INTEREST

Analysts need access. Analysts may be better than the rest of us at assessing the quality of a firm, but they also want to be better than the next analyst. To do this, analysts will try to obtain as much information as possible. Of course, the best source of a firm's information is the firm itself, and analysts want to be able to have frank discussions with the firm's management. This situation represents an obvious conflict of interest. How can an analyst who needs access to management turn around and give the firm a bad rating? Would the analyst be able to gain access again? One analyst said that without access, it becomes difficult to make quality stock assessments, akin to playing basketball with one hand tied behind your back.[8] In addition, because analysts typically specialize in a particular industry or two, they get to know the managers in the field. They may even develop friendships with them.

Specializing in a particular industry or sector allows the analyst to become an expert in the different influences and nuances of the industry. However, human nature tends to be optimistic, and this circumstance makes being objective difficult. Consider the predicament of an analyst following the airlines industry after the September 11, 2001, terrorist attack. The airlines clearly were going to experience both lower passenger demand and higher costs due to new regulations. Analysts rarely recommend selling all firms in the industry. Instead, they recommend buying the few companies that they think will hold up the best in a problematic industry. Therefore, investors may misinterpret a buy rating on a firm in a troubled industry.

ANALYSTS AT INVESTMENT BANKS

Analysts can work for an independent research firm, for a brokerage firm, or for the brokerage operation of an investment bank. Most high profile analysts who many investors follow work for investment banks.

Consider that investment banks have corporate clients who are also firms that their analysts follow. The fees for investment banking services can easily run into the tens of millions of dollars. Will these analysts feel free to make public honest assessments if it would jeopardize those banking fees? If an analyst came out with a negative rating, wouldn't the bankers be upset? If a non-client firm received a negative assessment from an analyst, that firm might not give the analyst's firm any investment banking business. Analysts that work at investment banks may feel the need to compromise their integrity for the good of their employer. Indeed, some analysts apparently have recommended stocks to the public that they personally thought were not good investments.

One academic study provides evidence consistent with this problem.[9] The study finds that stocks *promoted* by investment bank analysts where the institution recently provided services performed worse than stocks promoted by unaffiliated analysts. Also, according to a commentary in *Business Week*, the stock-picking performance of independent analyst firms such as Callard Asset Management and Alpha Equity Research outperformed the stock-picking performance of powerhouse investment banks such as Goldman Sachs, Solomon Smith Barney, Morgan Stanley, and Merrill Lynch.[10] This evidence suggests that conflicts of interest faced by analysts at investment banks may compromise some of their recommendations.

In the late 1990s, analysts more commonly became a part of the investment banking team. When bankers were pitching their services to a firm who wanted to issue securities, an analyst would be there. After the bankers were hired to underwrite the security, they took the analyst on the road show to help market the issue to institutional investors. In this capacity, analysts become salespeople and promoters of the firm instead of objective analyzers of financial performance.

BOX 6-2

EXAMPLE–MERRILL LYNCH: ANALYSTS VERSUS INVESTMENT BANKING

Merrill Lynch has been criticized for two apparent conflicts between analysts and investment banking in which the firm took the side of the bankers. The charge is that an analyst with a bearish recommendation on a firm was replaced with another analyst who was bullish to obtain investment banking business from the firm. Specifically, a more optimistic analyst replaced the previous analyst covering Enron in order to gain favor with Enron executives. Early in 1998, analyst John Olson recommended Enron stock with a "neutral" rating. Olson's negative rating and his personal style rubbed Enron executives Jeffrey Skilling and Ken Lay the wrong way. Merrill Lynch bankers complained to their CEO about not gaining any investment banking business with Enron while Olson rated the firm so poorly. The investment banking business kept going to banks where the analysts rated Enron as a "buy" or better. In August 1998, Olson left Merrill for another company Merrill then hired Donato Eassey to be the analyst covering Enron. Eassey quickly upgraded Enron to "accumulate." By the end of 1998, Merrill was providing investment banking services to Enron that would generate $45 million in fees.[11]

In another situation in 1999, Merrill replaced analyst Jeanne Terrile, who covered Tyco International, after Tyco CEO Dennis Kozlowski complained to Merrill CEO David Komansky.[12] The new analyst, Phua Young, promptly upgraded Tyco to a "buy" rating. The next year, Merrill underwrote Tyco's $3 billion stock issue. Both examples illustrate the strong power that public companies have over analysts who work at investment banks and the motivation of banks to be optimistic in order to gain underwriting business.

JUST WHO IS THE CLIENT?

From the point of view of the sell-side analyst, the public investor is not the client. The analyst's clients are those institutional or individual investors who trade through the firm's brokerage arm or who buy new security issues from the banking arm. In addition, analysts do not really consider the published ratings and earnings estimates to be the whole of their research product. Indeed, analysts do not just write a report and consider themselves done, rather they constantly revise their opinions and advise their biggest institutional clients. The public investor is not included in this process.

While this is the traditional role and duty of the analyst, the situation has substantially changed. If analysts just kept to their paying clients, then the public investor would not know about their recommendations, but this is not the case. Analysts market themselves and their firms to the public investor. Analysts commonly appear on TV networks like CNBC and CNNfn, and on TV shows with Lou Dobbs and Louis Rukeyser. When they make changes in their ratings, they alert the media. They also promote themselves and their ratings through numerous financial Web sites. Because analysts use the public to promote their own agendas, they must also be responsible to those investors.

CHANGING ROLES

The days of analysts aspiring for a piece of the investment banking action may be over. The National Association of Securities Dealers and the NYSE both put forth new or amended rules that would address the conflict of interest problem. The SEC approved these new regulations on May 10, 2002. Under the new rules, sell-side research analysts (1) cannot be subject to supervision from investment banking operations, (2) their compensation cannot be tied to investment banking deals, (3) and they cannot promise favorable ratings to lure investment-banking deals. Time will tell whether the new rules will help.

In May 2002, the SEC also told analysts to simplify their ratings to just three categories, buy, hold, sell. By September, the ratings had not changed much. The ratings were in only three categories, but only 7.5 percent were listed as sell. In addition, investment banking firm analysts still did not make sell ratings on firms who were also investment banking clients. For example, for every 25 firms Merrill Lynch had listed as a sell, only one was its client.[13] On the other hand, 60 percent of the companies receiving a buy rating were clients. At this time, a separation between analysts and banking has not effectively occurred.

❖ SUMMARY

Analysts evaluate a firm's performance and future prospects and then make trading recommendations. For the most part, they generally seem good at it. However, two conflicts of interest in the system may compromise their objectivity at times. First, analysts want to gather good information through access to the management team of the firm, which requires a good relationship. This might be difficult to do when the analyst thinks the firm's prospects are poor. Second, analysts have been rewarded for luring investment-banking business to their employer. Consequently, they were encouraged to be bullish on the firms they follow to keep both potential and current investment banking clients happy. Rules aimed at limiting these conflicts of interest have been passed. The SEC has also mandated that analysts certify that the opinions they express reflect their personal views. It may take some time before we know if these rules will work.

While we have focused on the problems in the analyst industry, there are many analysts trying to rectify some of these problems. The professional association of analysts, the Association of Investment Management Research (AIMR), already has been working with the SEC, Congress, and others to improve the integrity of analyst recommendations. Many of the new rules enacted by the SEC have been advocated by AIMR.

QUESTIONS

1. What is the financial analyst's function? How might analysts be important participants in the monitoring of the firm?

2. Why is it common for firms to beat analyst earnings expectations by a small margin?

3. Name and describe the conflicts of interest analysts face.

4. What value do analysts provide to their employers? To the public?

EXERCISES

1. Go to the AIMR Web site (*www.aimr.org*). Identify and describe the ideas that AIMR proposes to improve investor confidence in analyst recommendations. Evaluate the potential of these ideas for resolving the problems.

2. The actions of Jack Grubman, former analyst for Salomon Smith Barney, illustrate how conflicts of interest can create problems. He was later investigated by New York State Attorney General Eliot Spitzer. What was Grubman's role in the downfall of WorldCom? What was the outcome of Spitzer's investigation?

3. Barron's once dubbed Mary Meeker, a famous analyst at Morgan Stanley, "Queen of the Net" for her perpetual enthusiasm for Internet stocks no matter their valuations. Investigate her behavior during the bull market of the late 1990s and the bear market afterwards. What might have been her motives?

4. Pick a company and report its analyst's recommendations for trading and their predictions of future earnings. Is there a consensus among the analysts?

ENDNOTES

1. Stephanie Smith, "How are Analysts Changing?" *Money* (September 2002): 89.

2. Justin Fox, "Learn to Manage Your Earnings and Wall Street Will Love You," *Fortune* (March 31, 1997): 77–80.

3. Many academic articles have cited this phenomenon. For example, see Francois Degeorge, Jayendu Patel, and Richard J. Zeckhauser, "Earnings Management to Exceed Thresholds," *Journal of Business* 72 (1999).

4. Anup Agrawal and Sahiba Chadha, "Who Is Afraid of Reg FD? The Behavior and Performance of Sell-Side Analysts Following the SEC's Fair Disclosure Rules," unpublished paper available at *http://bama.ua.edu/aagrawal*.

5. Brad Barber, Reuven Lehavey, Maureen McNichols, and Brett Trueman, "Can Investors Profit from the Prophets? Security Analyst Recommendations and Stock Returns," *Journal of Finance* 56 (2001): 531–563.

6. Marcia Vickers and Mike France, "How Corrupt Is Wall Street?" *Business Week* (May 13, 2002): 37–42.

7. Mara De Hovanesian, " How Analysts' Pay Packets Got So Fat," *Business Week* (May 13, 2002): 40–41.

8. See endnote 6.

9. Roni Michaely and Kent L. Womack, "Conflict of Interest and the Credibility of Underwriter Analyst Recommendations," *Review of Financial Studies* 12 (1999): 653–686.

10. Emily Thornton, "Research Should Pay Its Own Way," *Business Week* (June 3, 2002): 72.

11. Olson, Eassey, and Merrill Lynch all deny that anything inappropriate occurred. Indeed, Eassey was one of the few analysts to downgrade Enron when its troubles began to become public. See Richard Oppel, "Merrill Replaced Research Analyst Who Upset Enron," *New York Times*, July 30, 2002, 1.1.

12. Charles Gasparino, "Merrill Replaced Its Tyco Analyst After Meeting," *Wall Street Journal*, September 17, 2002, C1.

13. Susanne Craig, "Securities Firms Do the Soft Sell in Their Ratings," *Wall Street Journal*, September 13, 2002, C1.

CHAPTER 7

CREDIT RATING AGENCIES

redit agencies can be considered as corporate system monitors. However, instead of focusing on protecting shareholders, credit agencies focus on protecting company bondholders and other creditors.

The safety level of a bond is very important to those who choose fixed-income investments. The very best return a bondholder can receive is both interest payments during the term of the bond and the principal upon maturity of the bond. Therefore, bondholders focus on safety. How do you know if a firm's debt is safe or risky? Corporate bonds are given a safety rating. At least one of four firms—Moody's Investors Service, Standard & Poor's, Dominion Bond Rating Service, and Fitch—conducts a credit analysis and gives the firm a grade. This grade informs investors about the risk of a bond. This chapter details the role of credit agencies in the corporate system and how they might occasionally fail in their responsibilities.

A BRIEF HISTORICAL PERSPECTIVE

A brief history will help the understanding of how the credit industry works and its importance. John Moody invented credit ratings in 1909 when he published a manual of ratings on 200 railroads and their securities.[1] He made his money by charging investors for the manual. By 1916, The Standard Company, the predecessor to Standard & Poor's, started rating bonds, and Fitch started rating bonds in 1920. By the 1970s, photocopy equipment was so prevalent that many investors obtained ratings without paying for the published books. However, the demand for the ratings was so great that rating companies could give the ratings free to investors and still earn money by charging the bond issuers fees to rate their bonds.

After the stock market crash of 1929 and the Great Depression, the government looked for ways to restore confidence in the banking system. The securities acts of 1933 and 1934 went a long way toward increasing regulation of the banking and securities industries. However, in 1936, the government expanded the role of credit ratings by requiring that commercial banks only hold high quality debt. Specifically, the Comptroller of the Currency decreed that banks could only own "investment-grade" bonds; this and other categories of ratings are illustrated in the next section. Because one large and influential type of investor (commercial banks) needed credit ratings on debt instruments in order to buy them, all bond issuers wanted to be rated. Today, anyone who wants to issue bonds in the United States needs to be rated. This applies to companies, state and local governments, and even foreign governments.

While the credit rating helps investors understand the riskiness of a bond issue, the company pays the bill. In other words, a company planning a bond issue could discuss it with several credit agencies and see which one would give them the highest grade. A high quality rating for a company means that they can offer bonds at a low interest rate and still easily sell them all. A lower quality rating would require offering the bonds at a higher interest rate, and it would cost the firm millions of dollars more in interest payments. Unscrupulous rating agencies could sell high ratings to firms willing to pay higher fees for them. In the wake of the 1975 scandalous bond default of Penn Central Corporation, the SEC designated three ratings agencies as the only ones satisfying rating regulations. The three anointed agencies, called Nationally Recognized Statistical Rating Organizations (NRSROs), were Moody's, Standard & Poor's, and Fitch. The SEC later designated four more agencies as valid, but mergers between the firms left only the three original firms. Then, in February 2003, the SEC approved a fourth firm, Dominion Bond Rating Service (of Canada). Nevertheless, having only four agencies creates an uncompetitive environment for the industry.

The situation of a small number of firms in an industry is called an *oligopoly*. The SEC rules protect the four firms from further competition by preventing any other firms from joining the industry. Other small credit agencies exist, but they must survive on the fees investors will pay for the evaluations. Finding substantial subscribers is difficult when the NRSROs provide free ratings. The SEC wants to give the designation to agencies that have large staffs and resources. Small credit rating agencies have tried and failed to obtain the SEC designation. These undesignated, small agencies find themselves in a catch-22. These firms cannot get the SEC designation until they are larger, but they cannot afford to grow without the fees they could charge with the designation.

With a lack of competition by new entrants, the four credit rating agencies operate very profitable businesses. The credit analysis process does not require expensive factories or machine tools. Low expenses and the low level of competition lead to high profits. Moody's profit margin is estimated to be 50 percent while Standard & Poor's is closer to 30 percent. These four firms have been immensely rewarded in the protected environment.

THE RATINGS

To assess the creditworthiness of companies, the credit agencies employ financial analysts who examine the firms' financial positions, business plans, and strategies. This means that the analysts carefully review public financial statements issued by the companies. To assist in their investigations, the SEC has granted the agencies an exemption from disclosure rules so that companies can reveal non-public or sensitive information to the agencies in confidence. Companies have no obligation to reveal special information, but they often do so to convince the agencies that their debt issues should be rated highly. Credit analysts can often question CEOs and other top executives directly when conducting reviews because of the importance of credit ratings.

The rating systems of Moody's and Standard & Poor's are shown in Table 7.1. Notice that the two ratings agencies have similar systems.[2] Also, both agencies can partition the ratings further. Moody's includes 1, 2, or 3 after the rating to show that the firm falls near the bottom, middle, or top of the scale within the category. Standard & Poor's uses a minus (–) or plus (+) sign. Consider two companies that want to borrow $1 billion by issuing bonds. The rating company rates the first company in the "high quality" category. This firm will have to pay 6.9 percent (or $69 million) in interest every year. The second firm is rated "non-investment grade" and would have to pay $99 million annually. These amounts differ substantially. Riskier companies pay higher interest.

If a company becomes financially stronger over time, then the bond rating will also improve. Therefore, the interest rate demanded by investors will fall, as illustrated in the table. When interest rates fall, bond prices rise. Consequently, if a firm becomes safer, then the price of its bonds will increase, which is what bondholders want. Alternatively, if the firm becomes riskier, then bond prices fall. The worst-case scenario for a bondholder is for the issuing company to default on the bonds and file for bankruptcy protection. Bondholders typically receive only a small portion of their principal back if a firm defaults.

TABLE 7.1   RATINGS OF BOND SAFETY AND EXAMPLE BOND YIELDS

	Moody's Rating	Standard & Poor's Rating	Example Bond Yield, %
Best Quality	Aaa	AAA	6.4
High Quality	Aa	AA	6.9
Upper Medium Grade	A	A	7.1
Medium Grade	Baa	BBB	7.8
Non-Investment Grade	Ba	BB	9.9
Highly Speculative	B	B	10.5
Defaulted or Close To It	Caa to C	CCC to D	20 to 90

The ratings that the four main credit agencies issue have historically been good predictors of the default potential of a debt issuer. Only 0.5 percent of firms rated at the highest level (best quality) default.[3] This percentage increases to only 1.3 percent for issuers rated as high quality. However, the increase in the default rate substantially increases to 19.5 percent in the non-investment-grade bonds and 54.4 percent in the CCC category.

When a firm begins to struggle financially, credit agencies downgrade the ratings on its securities. A bond issue rated AAA– might be downgraded to AA+ or even AA. If the business operations or cash position of the firm continues to decline, the rating could fall further. Each downgrade signals to investors that the bonds are becoming riskier. In response, the price of the bonds declines and investors experience a capital loss. The term "investment grade" in the regulations is interpreted as ratings of BBB– or higher. If a bond slips to BB+ or lower, it is not considered investment grade. In fact, the popular term for non-investment-grade bonds is junk bonds. For additional protection of a bondholder's principal, many modern debt offerings include a rule (or covenant) that requires the company to increase the interest payment made on the bonds if the rating slips to junk status. Some bond covenants require the company to pay back the principal if the rating slips to junk. While this sounds like a good idea for bond investors, in practice it often triggers the very bankruptcy filing that bondholders try to avoid. A firm's debt is downgraded to junk bond status because the company is having some financial difficulty. If the firm suddenly owes higher interest payments or even hundreds of millions of dollars in principal, it is pushed into a more financially precarious position. The very covenant rules that try to protect the interest of bondholders can actually drive a company toward insolvency.

CRITICISMS

One criticism of credit agencies is that they have started to enter the consulting business. Being both consultants and credit raters creates a conflict of interest similar to the one that occurred when auditing firms were also consultants for a company. If the credit agency is earning lucrative consulting fees, then it might not be able to provide unbiased analysis of the firm's financial position. Just as auditing firms should not be allowed to audit companies where they act as consultants, neither should credit agencies rate the debt securities of companies to which they provide consulting services.

A second criticism is that the credit agencies have been given the same First Amendment rights as the media. When disgruntled companies or investors have sued the credit agencies, agencies have been successful in using the free speech protection as a defense. The combination of regulated protection from new competitors, exemptions from disclosure rules, and First Amendment protection in court makes credit agencies nearly invincible, that is, market forces (such as competition) and the court system would have difficulty disciplining them.

BOX 7-1

EXAMPLE–JAPAN'S RATING

Credit rating agencies take criticism for rating decisions on individual issuers. Take, for example, the Moody's downgrade of Japan's government debt on May 31, 2002. The change in ratings took the grade down two notches to A2 from Aa3. Japanese government officials were furious at the move, and they argued that Japan had the second-largest economy in the world and the highest savings rate. The new debt rating suggested to investors that Japan's creditworthiness was on a par with that of Israel, South Africa, Poland, and Cyprus but below that of Hungary, Botswana, Chile, and the Czech Republic.[4] Officials argued that it was absurd for Japan's rating to be below that of developing countries to which Japan provided economic assistance.

While the total record of credit agencies is fairly accurate, they have made some dramatic mistakes. For example, the agencies completely missed the financial trouble and bankruptcy filing of Orange County, California, in 1994. In the early 1990s, the economic output of Orange County would have ranked it among the top 10 countries in the world. By every standard, the county was one of the wealthiest in the United States. As such, the credit agencies rated the municipal bonds of the county as very safe, a grade of AA.

Much of the money raised with bond issues in the county and elsewhere in California was invested by Orange County until it was needed to build a school, hospital, or other project. The county treasurer, Robert Citron, invested the funds. While municipal money investment is usually in very safe instruments, Citron used some complicated interest rate derivative securities that carried higher risks.[5] These risks became real to the county when they had to announce a "$1.5 billion paper loss" on December 1, 1994. On December 7, the county filed for bankruptcy protection. The credit rating agencies responded by downgrading many of the bonds from "high quality" to "close to default," quite a large downgrade! However, it was too late for bond investors. The agencies had rated the county as good investment-grade debt right up to the bankruptcy filing.

Another questionable call by the credit agencies occurred with the issuance of WorldCom bonds in May 2001. WorldCom issued an American record $11.9 billion of bonds, of which $10.1 billion was new financing. Standard & Poor's rated WorldCom and the massive debt issue investment grade, with a BBB+; Moody's rated it A3.[6] The massive offering by WorldCom should have come with a robust analysis by the investment banks, as the underwriters, and by the credit rating agencies.

One year later, in May 2002, the credit agencies downgraded WorldCom debt to junk-bond status. The rationale behind the downgrade was that WorldCom's total debt of $30 billion was too high.[7] Why were the agencies unconcerned with the debt level the previous year when WorldCom increased its debt by 50 percent with the massive bond issue? The agencies' initial seal of approval on the giant bond issue and the company downgrade one year later based on that same issue seems hard to believe. The high rating by the agencies allowed WorldCom to borrow that much money in the first place. The next month, on June 25, 2002, WorldCom disclosed that it had improperly booked $3.8 billion as capital investments instead of operating expenses over the previous five quarters. It found several more billion in accounting fraud over the next couple of months.

Credit agencies are not blameless in the corporate scandals of 2001 and 2002. Indeed, their special relationships with companies allows them to obtain private information that other monitors, such as independent analysts, might not receive. Of the outside monitors, credit rating agencies might have been in the best position to detect corporate fraud and warn investors. Yet, in some cases, these groups were one of the last to respond.

BOX 7-2

EXAMPLE–ENRON

The price of a share of Enron stock was $90 in August 2000, but by April 2001 the stock price had fallen to $60 per share. In the late summer, the price continued to fall and reached less than $40 per share. Even in November 2001, just before Enron declared bankruptcy, the stock had declined to less than $5 per share. This decline in Enron's stock price should have been a big warning that something was drastically amiss. As it turned out, the credit agencies might have been more enablers than watchdogs.

The investment banks had raised capital for Enron's offshore partnerships, which Enron used to falsify loans as profits. The banks had invested hundreds of millions of dollars of their own money in Enron and its associated partnerships. The banks knew that if Enron filed for bankruptcy protection, their losses would be enormous. The banks also knew that if the credit rating agencies were to downgrade Enron to non-investment grade status, at least $3.9 billion in debt repayment would immediately be required. Enron would be forced to declare itself insolvent.

On November 8, 2001, the news about the partnerships and the massive losses became public. The stock price went down to less than $10 per share. The banks needed to act quickly or take massive losses; they wanted the credit agencies to hold off on their downgrade while they looked for new capital with which to save Enron.

Apparently, the credit agencies delayed in downgrading Enron to non-investment grade. At first, they merely downgraded the firm to the lowest levels of investment-grade ratings. Because companies seek a rating on debt they issue and investment banks help them issue the debt securities, banks and credit agencies frequently work together. The bankers may have used this relationship to convince the credit agencies to give them some time to save Enron.

To locate a buyer, investment banks Merrill Lynch and J.P. Morgan looked across town from the headquarters of Enron and found Dynegy. Enron and Dynegy executives began merger negotiations in November 2001. If they could agree, Dynegy would infuse Enron with $1.5 billion of cash to tide them over until the final merger could take place. The credit rating agencies knew that if the merger did not take place, Enron would be in deep financial trouble. Yet, instead of communicating this enormous risk to bondholders via a downgrade to junk bond status, the agencies waited. Given what the agencies knew, this situation was a big gamble for bondholders, like flipping a coin. Heads the merger goes through and the financial situation improves, tails it does not and Enron probably goes into bankruptcy. Investors might take this risk in speculative stocks but not in investment-grade bonds. The stock price had fallen to less than $5 per share. The credit rating agencies failed to warn investors how risky the situation had become.

On November 26, the Enron merger with Dynegy was dead. Enron was still discovering how vast the partnership problems were becoming. The designated credit rating agencies downgraded Enron to junk bond status on November 28. Enron's stock price fell to $0.61 per share. On December 2, 2001, Enron filed for bankruptcy protection. Bondholders waited in line at bankruptcy court with other creditors and hoped to regain some of their principal.

When NRSRO-designated agencies do make mistakes, they often claim the company executives lied to them. However, the agency's job is to validate the information they receive and then make conclusions based on its own analysis. What purpose do agencies serve as independent monitors if they simply follow the lead of the company executives?

❖ SUMMARY

The credit agency's purpose is monitoring debt issuers to protect public investors. However, the industry's structure creates a situation in which the agencies interact only a little with the investors they are protecting. Instead, debt issuers pay agencies to give a rating. Agencies work with the issuers and the investment bankers to obtain information about the debt issue. Most of their business relies on the interactions with corporate participants, not with investors. In this process, they gain access to private information about the firm. Overall, the NRSRO-designated agencies have done a good job of showing bond investors the level of risk they take in various bond issues.

Most of the agencies' interactions, and the fees they earn, are with the firms they rate, not the investors who use the ratings. This circumstance can create misaligned incentives. In addition, the U.S. government has made credit rating a closed and noncompetitive industry that seems to have unusual immunity under the First Amendment in the court system. This immunity prevents investors from seeking damages when the agencies make mistakes. The lack of disciplinary market and legal forces can make the agencies lax in their watchdog duties.

QUESTIONS

1. How are credit rating agencies important for firms, investors, and investment banks?

2. Why is the distinction between investment grade and non investment grade ratings so important?

3. The SEC awards the Nationally Recognized Statistical Rating Organization designation. What criteria do they use to give the designation?

4. How did the rating agencies fail Enron bondholders and creditors?

5. Name and describe the conflicts of interest that credit agencies face.

EXERCISES

1. There are only four NRSRO-designated rating firms. What might be done to increase the number of rating firms?

2. Obtain the ratings from all four credit rating firms for one company. Compare the ratings.

3. Obtain the credit ratings for a firm over the past five years. How and why has the rating changed?

ENDNOTES

1. Amy Borrus, Mike McNamee, and Heather Timmons, "The Credit-Raters: How They Work and How They Might Work Better," *Business Week* (April 8, 2002):38.

2. Ratings categories are from *www.moodys.com* and *www.standardandpoors.com*.

3. Standard & Poor's estimates use data from 1987–2001.

4. Akiko Kashiwagi, "Japan's Credit Rating Cut by Two Notches," *Washington Post*, June 1, 2002, E1; and Valerie Reitman, "Asia: Moody's Downgrade Infuriates the Government, Which Had Protested the Action," *Los Angeles Times*, June 1, 2002, C1.

5. John Nofsinger, *Investment Blunders of the Rich and Famous* (Upper Saddle River, NJ: Financial Times Prentice Hall, 2002).

6. "WorldCom Smashes Records with $11.9bn Blowout Bond," *Euroweek*, May 11, 2001, 4.

7. Gregory Zuckerman and Shawn Young, "Leading the News: WorldCom Debt Is Slashed to 'Junk'," *Wall Street Journal*, May 10, 2002, A3.

CHAPTER 8

THE SECURITIES AND EXCHANGE COMMISSION

For a while, everyone enjoyed a tremendous bull market. Business seemed to be booming. Investors speculated in the stock markets, optimism was high, and some people even pondered early retirement. Then suddenly, quite dramatically, all of it changed. Large corporations went bankrupt. Corporate officers were found to be deceiving the public. Executives became engaged in courtroom battles that grabbed national headlines. As a result, investors were leery of corporations, and the stock markets plummeted.

While these events may sound like the late 1990s and early 2000s, they also describe the late 1920s and early 1930s. This period spawned the Great Depression. There are many examples of fraudulent behavior that can be used to illustrate those times, including unethical activities by corporate executives, securities analysts, large investors, and even newspaper reporters who hyped their own stocks. Instead of dwelling on these examples, knowing that our nation has experienced these events before is enough.

What did the United States do to try to fix the crisis during the early 1930s? The government did something quite dramatic; it decided to regulate the securities markets and created the Securities and Exchange Commission (SEC). The SEC would become the investor's advocate, putting investors on equal footing with the corporations in which they invest. When President Franklin D. Roosevelt signed the Securities Act of 1933 into law, he stated, "The Act is thus intended to correct some of the evils which have been so glaringly revealed in the private exploitation of the public's money."[1] Seventy years later, the nation finds itself again in the midst of an investor confidence crisis.

Corporations in the United States are regulated by many governmental agencies. For example, the Fair Trade Commission (FTC) regulates advertising by businesses and the Food and Drug Administration (FDA) approves pharmaceutical company drug sales, all to protect consumers. What makes the SEC different from other business overseers is its role of protecting investors. Therefore, the SEC is a very important component of the corporate governance system. This chapter provides an overview of the SEC, and it outlines some of its difficulties in effectively carrying out its monitoring role.

THE SECURITIES ACTS

There are seven major laws that govern the securities industry, which the SEC oversees. The first is the Securities Act of 1933. This act requires firms to register securities intended for public sale. In the registration, important information regarding the securities for sale and the firm (e.g., its financial statements, its business operations, and its management) must be disclosed. No information can be fraudulent or deceitful. All statements are made publicly available.

The Securities Exchange Act of 1934 created the SEC and gave it authority to oversee the securities industry, including large shareholders (defined as 5 percent shareholders), brokerage firms, securities dealers, and the stock exchanges. Corporations are required to submit accurate annual reports (also known as 10-Ks) and quarterly reports (also known as 10-Qs). The act also allows the SEC to govern the proxy process (this is the process used to solicit shareholder votes) and insider trading. This act, along with the Securities Act of 1933, was specifically designed to restore investor confidence.

The Trust Indenture Act of 1939 applies to the sale and formal agreement between buyer and seller of debt securities. The Investment Company Act of 1940 regulates investment companies such as mutual funds by requiring the disclosure of their financial condition and their investment policies. The Investment Advisors Act of 1940 currently regulates investment advisors who manage more than $25 million or who advise a registered investment company. Finally, the Public Utility Holding Company Act of 1935 regulates gas and electric holding companies.

In the summer of 2002, the Sarbanes-Oxley Act, otherwise known as the Public Company Accounting Reform and Investor Protection Act of 2002, was signed into law. This new law sets up a new oversight body to regulate auditors, creates laws pertaining to corporate responsibility, and increases punishments for corporate white-collar criminals. The main aspects of this act follow.

1. The legislation establishes a nonprofit corporation called the Public Company Accounting Oversight Board, which will operate under SEC discretion, to oversee the audit of public companies and to protect the interests of investors and the general public by improving audit report accuracy.
2. The act attempts to protect investors by breaking the relationships among auditors, consultants, and the public company being audited.

3. The act increases the monitoring ability and responsibilities of boards of directors and improves their credibility by making boards more independent and more responsible for audits.
4. The act tries to make executive actions more transparent to shareholders by requiring the disclosure of "off-balance-sheet transactions" and decreasing the time to two days that an executive has to report company stock (and other equity) trades to the SEC.
5. The legislation makes it easier to prosecute executive criminal behavior in the future by spelling out new or altered definitions of criminal behaviors, and it stiffens penalties.

Note that all of the acts taken together, especially the first two and the last one, boil down to the following: The acts force corporations to tell the public about themselves, and they cannot lie. This way, investors can then make informed decisions. In addition, the spirit of the acts is to put investors' interests first.

ORGANIZATIONAL STRUCTURE OF THE SEC

Headquartered in Washington, D.C., the SEC has 11 regional and district offices, including those in Chicago, Denver, Los Angeles, and New York City. The commission consists of 4 divisions and 18 offices and employs almost 3,000 people.

At the top of the organizational chart are the commissioners. Five commissioners each serve a five-year term; the U.S. president appoints these people and the Senate must approve them. Appointments occur annually, and there is one appointment per year because the terms are staggered. No more than three commissioners can belong to the same political party. One commissioner serves as chairman, the top SEC executive, and is also designated by the president.

Figure 8.1 shows the four divisions that are the pillars of the SEC. The Division of Corporate Finance oversees corporate disclosure, ensuring that the public has all relevant information necessary to make investment decisions. Full corporate disclosure encompasses the registration statements of securities for sale, annual and quarterly reports, proxy materials, and annual reports to shareholders. The Division of Market Regulation oversees securities markets participants, such as the brokerage firms and their agents, and the stock exchanges. The Division of Investment Management primarily regulates investment companies. Finally, the Division of Enforcement investigates possible violations of securities laws. The SEC has only civil enforcement authority, but it can also play a crucial role in helping federal agencies pursue criminal charges for severe violations of the law. Each year, the SEC prosecutes between 400 and 500 individuals and companies for wrongdoing, with most of these prosecutions being settled out of court. These violations mainly involve accounting fraud, insider trading, and deception regarding securities.

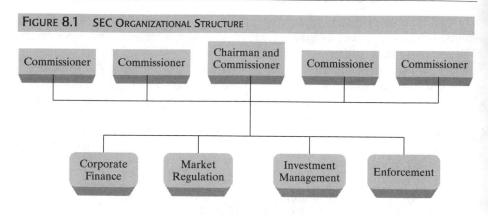

FIGURE 8.1   SEC ORGANIZATIONAL STRUCTURE

The 18 offices mostly deal with SEC internal affairs, such as personnel, or serve as advisors (e.g., general counsel and economists) for the divisions and the SEC commissioners. The other responsibilities of these offices are varied, including the handling of compliance inspections, investor education, and international affairs.

NEED FOR THE ACTS AND THE SEC

Opinions regarding the SEC vary. Businesses and the securities industry are not always happy with SEC decisions. The costs of reporting and following SEC regulations, in general, are tremendous. Byron C. Radaker, CEO of Congoleum Corporation, took his company private in the early 1980s, citing that this would save his firm between $6 and $8 million dollars per year in reporting costs.[2] While companies may not appreciate the SEC, can investors do without it? In order to consider this, first think about the thrust of the Securities Acts.

Many people, especially academics, believe that the stock markets are "efficient." What does this mean? The notion of market efficiency is that current stock prices reflect their correct value. To understand this concept, consider this point: Millions of people participate in the stock markets. The average of their beliefs and opinions, based on current and past information, will be reflected in the current stock price. For example, if a stock price is too low, some people out of the millions would recognize this and rush to buy the stock. Because of the buying, the stock price would rise and not be undervalued for long. Millions of market participants continuously process information, which, in turn, makes the markets efficient. If markets are efficient, then do we really need the SEC?

In the context of market efficiency, if companies do hide facts or lie, then someone will find out because many people are involved, including brokers, analysts, directors, employees, accountants, creditors, investors, and even state regulators.

Thus, the inevitable revelation of fraud will cause the stock price to plummet. Besides, companies that lie and get caught cannot last anyway. We have always had a climate where consumers and investors have cast a suspicious eye toward big businesses.

Some finance scholars have attempted to assess empirically the importance of SEC regulation to our financial markets. In 1964, George Stigler, who would later go on to win the Nobel Prize in economics, published a famous study in which he compared new securities being issued in the 1920s to those issued in the 1950s to determine whether the existence of the SEC had improved the securities markets.[3] He found no difference, and he contended that SEC regulation did not improve the quality of the securities markets. However, Professors Irwin Friend and Edward S. Herman subsequently debunked Stigler's study, citing that securities fraud decreased because of the existence of the SEC.[4] This debate continues today. In 1995, in response to market participants' complaints regarding regulatory costs and excessive regulatory burdens, the SEC formed a committee to study the feasibility of making it less burdensome for established public firms to issue securities.[5] In 1998, the SEC issued such a proposal, but it was not enacted.

Overall, we may never know for sure if the SEC does make our securities markets better. Perhaps markets would still be efficient without the SEC. However, the very existence of the SEC might contribute to making our markets efficient.

SEC PROBLEM AREAS

One issue that people wonder about is the adequacy of quarterly and annual reporting. If the information is to be useful, then there may need to be more frequent reporting. We now live in a world where technology permits us to access information, especially up-to-date information, on a continuous basis. Why not take advantage of this? Of course, frequent reporting would cause an outcry by corporate America, which already complains about reporting costs, but there may be several viable ways to address this issue. One approach currently under consideration is to require companies to submit their reports earlier.[6] Instead of providing a deadline of 90 days after the close of the fiscal year for filing of annual reports, it could be 60 days. For quarterly filings, the deadline could be shortened to 30 days instead of 45. However, this suggestion might not be ideal. Note that the report frequency may still be the same, but the timeliness would improve. Also, as pointed out in a *Business Week* commentary, this proposal might only add concerns about the hastiness, and thus the accuracy, with which companies compile reports.[7] Another way to address the problem of infrequent reporting (one also currently being considered) is to force companies to reveal immediately any material information that investors will deem important.[8] Such information could include the selling and buying of stocks by insiders; it currently can take many months before such reporting is filed.

Others believe that the SEC may be too weak because it cannot pursue criminal prosecution. Note that the SEC has the authority to bring civil charges only. If criminal prosecution can serve as a key deterrent to corporate crime, then there may be some truth to the notion that the SEC does not really have the policing power necessary to do its job. However, this problem may not be critical. The SEC can easily persuade prosecutors to bring criminal charges once it has evidence that the case has merit. Also, keep in mind that prosecuting corporate criminals is difficult. As pointed out in the July 1, 2002, issue of *Business Week,*[9] securities laws are ambiguous, sophisticated financial concepts that are difficult to grasp, and executives have plenty of tricks up their sleeves to absolve themselves of responsibility (e.g., "I didn't know that the books were fraudulent."). Therefore, in light of current difficulties with criminal charges, giving an additional agency such as the SEC the additional responsibility of bringing criminal charges might not make sense.

Another problem may be that the commission is under-funded. Being underfunded has two repercussions. First, the SEC may be hindered in its ability to hire and retain the best staff. One estimate puts the pay of SEC attorneys and examiners at as much as 40 percent less than their peers at comparable federal agencies.[10] In 2001, Congress did give approval to the SEC to pay its lawyers and accountants salaries that are competitive with other government banking agencies, such as the Federal Reserve. The increase in budget from the passage of the Public Company Accounting Reform and Investor Protection Act of 2002 ended up being much larger, more than $300 million, than the previous budget. For a long time, the SEC has had the distinction of being an important stepping-stone for many young ambitious and talented attorneys and accountants, who usually can count on the experience to command much higher salaries elsewhere. These talented people gain experience and a name for themselves at the SEC, and then they are hired by the very law firms that represent companies, auditing firms, and individuals that deal with the SEC. According to one estimate, the SEC employee turnover rate is 30 percent, which is double the rate for the rest of the government. Losing talent shortens the SEC's institutional memory and the average experience of its key employees while it increases the time and money needed to train new hires.

Another repercussion of being under-funded is being understaffed. Since 1993, the SEC's workload has increased by 80 percent but staffing levels have been stagnant.[11] Former SEC Commissioner Laura S. Unger once admitted that there were only about 100 lawyers that reviewed the disclosure documents of the 17,000 public firms.[12] An SEC chief accountant stated that only 1 out of 15 annual reports is reviewed. While it may be impossible for the SEC ever to be able to pursue and investigate thoroughly all possible violations, a larger staff would definitely be able to do more. In light of the recent crisis, the SEC has tripled the number of probes.[13] However, overworking the current staff cannot last forever. Fortunately, the Public Company Accounting Reform and Investor Protection Act of 2002 mandated that the SEC hire hundreds more people. Of course, it takes time to hire, train, and effectively use so many new employees.

BOX 8-1

EXAMPLE–ARTHUR LEVITT'S I TOLD YOU SO

Arthur Levitt served as SEC chairman from 1993 to 2001, and he was often criticized by business—both corporate America and the accounting profession attacked him. This situation is probably why a September 2000 issue of *Business Week* dubbed Levitt the "Investor's Champion."[14]

Levitt was known as a tough regulator whose victories included censuring the National Association of Securities Dealers for collusive pricing practices, which resulted in Nasdaq dealers having to pony up more than $1 billion to settle the case. Another was the adoption of Regulation Fair Disclosure, which put an end to corporate officers tipping off analysts. Toward the end of his tenure, one of his main causes was to clean up the accounting profession. In a famous speech delivered at New York University on September 28, 1998, Levitt called for an end to the "numbers game."[15] Levitt felt that corporate managers, auditors, and analysts participated in the process of managing earnings, using a variety of tricks (he called them "nods and winks") to meet earnings estimates, all at the expense of high quality full disclosure. He felt that this game had to stop, and accountants needed to make numbers more reliable and to have the trust of the investing public.

Levitt felt strongly that one way to clean up the accounting profession, which in the late 1990s was facing a slew of accounting scandals, would be to separate the accountant's role as auditor and consultant for the same firm. Levitt felt that this was a huge conflict of interest. Of course, there was a tremendous backlash from both corporate America, which claimed that accountants who consult for them are in the best position to audit them, and from the accounting industry, which did not want to see profitable consulting practices taken away. Less than two years later, on June 27, 2000, the SEC unanimously approved issuing Levitt's proposal. In the end, Congress defeated the proposal. Then two years later, Congress passed most of Levitt's proposals in the Sarbanes-Oxley Act of 2002. Senator Robert Torricelli, a New Jersey democrat, told Levitt on January 24, 2002, "We were wrong. You were right."[16]

❖ **SUMMARY**

The SEC's main function is to oversee the federal securities acts, which mandate that public corporations tell the public about themselves and that they do so honestly. Therefore, the SEC is an important corporate monitor; in fact, this work is its explicit designated function. However, the SEC has encountered some problems in the performance of its duties. Increasing the SEC's budget and hiring new employees will surely increase enforcement in the short term, but only for the short term. Years from now, after investor confidence has been restored, who is to say that those budgets will not be cut back again? The government tends to spend money where the public and the media have its attention and cut budgets elsewhere. In the 1990s, the number of investors in the stock market quadrupled, but the SEC budget hardly budged. In 1996, a Senate committee initially tried to cut the SEC budget by 20 percent, but it eventually kept the budget at the existing level. In 1998, Chairman Levitt appealed to Congress for an emergency $7 million for special bonuses to stem the high turnover of SEC attorneys and investigators. Congress rejected the proposal. Finally, in 2001, Congress did agree to increase the SEC budget but never appropriated all the money for the increase. What will happen to the SEC budget, and its ability to regulate, several years from now when the public focus has moved elsewhere?

QUESTIONS

1. Name and describe the acts that are overseen by the SEC, which governs the securities industry.
2. Describe the structure and functions of the SEC.
3. What are the main problems that the SEC has encountered in trying to perform its duties?

EXERCISES

1. Who are the current SEC commissioners, and who is the chairman?
2. Go to the SEC Web site (*www.sec.gov*). Go to the regulatory actions link and describe some of the proposed and final rule changes. Why are they being implemented?
3. Go to the enforcement division link at the SEC Web site and summarize some of the civil actions taken by the SEC.
4. Investigate and report on the progress of setting up the new Public Company Accounting Company Oversight Board. Has it started functioning? What are its priorities?

ENDNOTES

1. Joel Seligman, *The Transformation of Wall Street*, (Boston, MA: Northeastern University Press, 1995).
2. Cited in Eugene F. Brigham and Michael C. Ehrhardt, *Financial Management*, 10th Edition. Harcourt Publishers, Orlando, FL, (2002):759.
3. George J. Stigler, "Public Regulation of the Securities Markets," *Journal of Business* 37 (1964):117–142.
4. Irwin Friend and Edward S. Herman, "The SEC Through a Glass Darkly," *Journal of Business* 37 (1964):382–405.
5. See unpublished paper by Hyun-Han Shin, "The SEC's Review of the Registration Statement and Stock Price Movements during the Seasoned Equity Issuance Process," (Ph.D. diss., Ohio State University, 1995).
6. Judy Mathewson, James L. Tyson, and David Evans, "Harvey Pitt: Odd Man Out on Enron," *Bloomberg Markets* (March 2002):51–56.
7. Mike McNamee, "The SEC's Accounting Reforms Won't Answer Investor's Prayers," *Business Week* (June 17, 2002):28.
8. See note 6 above.
9. Mike France and Dan Carney, "Why Corporate Crooks Are Tough to Nail," *Business Week* (July 1, 2002):35–38.

10. Joseph Nocera, "System Failure," *Fortune* (June 24, 2002):62–72.
11. Mike McNamee and Amy Borrus, "The Reluctant Reformer," *Business Week* (March 25, 2002):72–81.
12. See note 10 above.
13. See note 11 above.
14. Cover story in *Business Week* (September 25, 2000).
15. The full text of Levitt's speech is available on *www.rutgers.edu/raw/aaa/newarc*.
16. See note 6 above.

CHAPTER 9

SHAREHOLDER ACTIVISM

When corporate scandals occur, shareholders are often viewed as the innocent and helpless victims. Investors may be categorized in two groups: individual investors and institutional investors, such as pension funds, insurance companies, and mutual funds. Many institutional investors actually invest on behalf of many smaller individual investors. Shareholders, both individuals and institutions, have expressed a desire for more protection. This very desire for more protection has everyone, from the stock exchanges to the SEC, trying to find ways to protect investors. However, one question that begs asking is, why can't shareholders *also* take care of themselves? That is, why do they not take more responsibility for the stocks that they own?

People who own homes will often take precautions to safeguard themselves against burglary. Various ways to protect a home range from forming neighborhood watches, buying a watchdog, or installing a security system to simply locking the doors each night before going to bed. Of course, homeowners also rely on the local police to protect their homes, but the police obviously cannot guarantee that all homes will be perfectly protected. This is just as true with shareholders' stocks.

There are valid reasons why individual investors do not pay more attention to what they own. Most individual shareholders do not own enough stock in any one company to be able to influence its management. Nor do most shareholders think it worth their time and effort to do anything. The gains (e.g., stock price increases) from their efforts would be shared by all other shareholders, while they alone would suffer the costs. If shareholders do anything at all, they sell shares that they are unhappy with, commonly known as doing the "Wall Street walk."

Institutional shareholders that own many different stocks have some restrictions about what they can own and, for them, exerting some of their ownership rights may be worthwhile. Further, given the large amounts of stocks that these shareholders own, they may be able to affect the decision-making of the firm. Also, the potential benefits accrued from their activism may be large enough to be worth the effort. Perhaps institutional shareholders can do more, especially given the fact that individuals have entrusted them to invest their money. According to the Survey of Consumer Finances, more individuals own stocks through a fund than own stocks directly. In 1998, for example, 50.2 million individuals owned stocks through a fund as compared with 33.8 million individuals who only owned stock directly. Therefore, institutional shareholder activism could play an important role in monitoring management.

This chapter discusses investor activism of various forms, including ways that individual shareholders can exert some influence over the firms that they own. The focus, however, will be on activism by institutional shareholders. Problems and constraints that institutional shareholders currently face are also described.

WHAT IS SHAREHOLDER ACTIVISM?

There is no formal definition of shareholder activism. Loosely speaking, any time shareholders express their opinions to try to affect or to influence a firm they are being active shareholders. Shareholders who vote their shares, submit proposals to be voted on, or attend annual shareholder meetings could certainly be considered active. Even writing a letter to management regarding some aspect of the firm's operations or social policies could be considered investor activism. For example, Lee Greenwood is an active shareholder well-known to General Mills management. Greenwood once simply suggested that Wheaties® should appear on airlines and in hotels.[1] Among individual shareholder activists, however, Evelyn Y. Davis is perhaps the most well-known and has been featured in *People* magazine.[2] As the modest shareholder of about 120 firms, Davis attends about 40 shareholder meetings each year. What does she do at these meetings? As everyone from journalists to executives seems to put it, she "raises hell." Davis has berated executives for everything from questionable merger decisions to the enormous size of their pay. Most individual shareholder activists use less dramatic methods. However, enough people like Evelyn Davis vigorously and frequently make themselves heard to have been deemed "corporate gadflies."

Lewis Gilbert is generally credited with being the first individual shareholder activist.[3] In 1932, as the owner of 10 shares of New York's Consolidated Gas Company, he attended its annual meeting. While at the meeting, he was appalled that he was not given a chance to ask questions. Subsequently, Gilbert and his brother pushed for reform, and, in 1942, the SEC created a rule to allow shareholders to submit proposals that could be put to a vote. Today, most shareholder proposals are governance-oriented, primarily attempting to forge an alignment between shareholder views and managerial actions. For example, proposals may address issues related to anti-takeover amendments, shareholder voting rules, or board composition.[4] Having these proposals passed, or even brought to the attention of the managers, can certainly have a potentially positive effect on the firm.

In practice, most shareholder proposals do not pass, especially those that go against management desires and those that involve obtaining a board seat. One reason is that it is difficult and expensive for one shareholder to communicate with all other shareholders. Also, most passive shareholders are reluctant to vote against the firm's management.

BOX 9-1

EXAMPLE–INDIVIDUAL INVESTOR ACTIVISM

During 2000, Computer Associates (CA) stock price had dropped from a $70 high in January to about $30 in September. In the following year, Sam Wyly sponsored a proposal to unseat four CA board members.[5] After a highly publicized and expensive campaign, Wyly's proposal was defeated, primarily because it also sought to unseat the firm's cofounder and board chairman, Charles Wang. This example does not mean, however, that proposals, and even defeats, are fruitless or that shareholders should give up. Robert A.G. Monks spent $250,000 to run for a board seat at Sears in 1991. His effort resulted in defeat, but the publicity eventually caused Sears to make massive changes on its own.[6]

Proposals do sometimes gain majority support. John Chevedden sponsored a proposal in 2001 to change the way board members are elected at Airborne Freight, and he gained support of 71 percent of the voting shareholders.[7] During that same year, Guy Adams beat tremendous odds with his bid for a board seat. As the owner of 1,100 shares of Lone Star restaurant stock, or 0.005 percent of the company, he was disgruntled because his stock had plummeted in value while the CEO's income rose. Consequently, Adams ran for a board seat, one held by the restaurant CEO Jamie B. Coulter. Despite the fact that Adams had never before served on a corporate board and had no restaurant experience, Adams actually won. What does he plan to do with his newfound authority and power? He says he will be a watchdog for other Lone Star investors.[8] Is that not what all the board members should be doing?

Institutional shareholders have the potential to exert effective influence. One academic study finds that proposals sponsored by institutional shareholders have a much greater chance of success than ones sponsored by individuals.[9]

Fortunately, institutional shareholders, especially public pension funds, have become more active in their oversight of companies. One reason for their increased activity is their increasing ownership stakes. The pie charts in Figures 9.1 and 9.2 show the percent of U.S. equities held by different shareholder types for the years 1970 and 2001.[10]

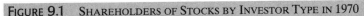

FIGURE 9.1   SHAREHOLDERS OF STOCKS BY INVESTOR TYPE IN 1970

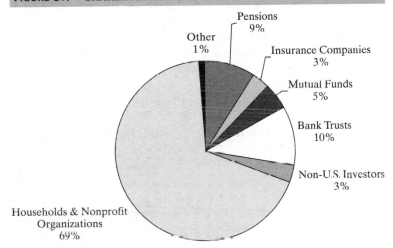

FIGURE 9.2   SHAREHOLDERS OF STOCKS BY INVESTOR TYPE IN 2001

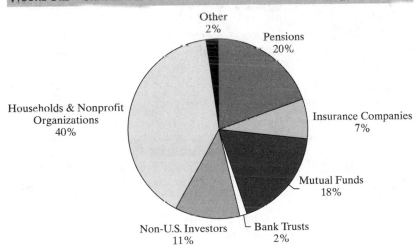

From these charts, one can see that institutions now own a larger percentage of shares than they did in 1970. The most dramatic increases are with pension funds and mutual funds. In fact, according to John Bogle, retired founder of Vanguard, just 75 funds held 44 percent of the U.S. stock market at one point during 2001.[11] As such, these funds do have the economic incentive to be more active, and some actually have been.

Further, note that both pension funds and mutual funds actually manage money on behalf of many smaller investors. As such, the individual investor has a right to push institutions to be more active shareholders. This may be especially true of pension funds, which have fewer restrictions on how much of a firm they can own. Pensions can take on a relatively large ownership stake and subsequently engage in a long-term active ownership role in the firm. Under the Employee Retirement Income Security Act (ERISA), pension funds have a fiduciary responsibility to their plan participants and beneficiaries. Therefore, not surprisingly, public pension funds often lead the way with regard to institutional shareholder activism.

Since the early 1990s, a few public pension funds have taken on a relational investor role with a long-run mindset. These funds have tried to influence the firms they own mainly through direct communication with management and other shareholders, by identifying poor corporate performers, and through pushing for reforms.[12] For example, the public pension fund California Public Employees' Retirement System (CalPERS), which has $100 billion in assets and serves one million members, has targeted Sears and Westinghouse in the past and has pushed for them to divest laggard divisions. Also, during July 2002, the chairmen of 1,754 major U.S. firms all received a letter from the Teachers Insurance and Annuity Association College Retirement Equities Fund (TIAA-CREF), the country's largest pension fund, asking them to account for stock options as an expense.[13] Activism by TIAA-CREF is quite common; they constantly monitor firms and make numerous recommendations for reform.

To help increase their influence, many pension funds belong to a coalition called the Council of Institutional Investors (CII), whose primary objective is to help members take an active role in protecting their assets. Given that pension funds control more than $1 trillion worth of assets, they certainly do have an incentive to come together and exert influence.

DOES INSTITUTIONAL SHAREHOLDER ACTIVISM WORK?

Determining whether activism bears positive results is difficult because, more often than not, good subsequent firm performance cannot be directly linked to increased activism. According to one study commissioned by CalPERS, Steven

Nesbitt of Wilshire Associates conducted a before and after analysis of 42 firms targeted for reform by CalPERS. After being targeted, the aggregate stock returns of these 42 firms over a five-year period were 52.5 percent higher than the returns of the S&P 500 Index. Prior to being targeted, these same firms had under performed the S&P 500 by 66 percent over a five-year period.[14] Michael P. Smith of the Economic Analysis Corporation conducted an independent study of CalPERS' activism, and he found that the combined gain to CalPERS for their activities related to 34 targeted firms was $19 million during the 1987 to 1993 period while the total cost to their monitoring was only $3.5 million.[15] His evidence also suggests that CalPERS' activism works.

However, counter evidence also exists. In one academic study, the authors found that shareholder proposal submission did not lead to any obvious improvements in firm performance, even for those firms where the proposals passed.[16] In a study that examined the effects of targeting by CII, the authors found no subsequent improvement for the targeted firms and very little evidence of the efficacy of shareholder activism.[17] Due to the inconsistent evidence, whether activism really changes firms for the better is unknown. Perhaps one of the main problems is that activism has its own set of shortcomings.

POTENTIAL ROADBLOCKS TO EFFECTIVE SHAREHOLDER ACTIVISM

Mutual funds and pension funds try to earn a high return on their portfolios. However, many active investors have a speculative or short-run view of the stock markets, and they make trading and investment decisions based on short-term trends. The short-term view of these investors limits their desire to be activists.

Institutional investors might be interested in good performance for the short term and then selling the stock to move on to something else. John Bogle makes the same contention; he has been calling on mutual fund managers to engage in more activism, but instead he witnesses mutual funds engaging in speculative investing. Bogle claims that during 2001, 4 out of every 10 equity funds turned their portfolio over at an annual rate of more than 100 percent.[18] If the equity funds do not like the future prospects of a firm, they simply sell the stock instead of working to change the firm.

In some cases, activist investors even enabled corporate problems. There were some reports that CalPERS had known about Andrew S. Fastow's questionable self-dealing partnerships with Enron but remained silent.[19] Indeed, CalPERS invested $250 million in Enron's offshore partnership JEDI.[20] Later, CalPERS invested more money in the partnership JEDI II. How could an institutional investor trying to champion proper corporate behavior neglect an obvious conflict of interest? Perhaps the reason was CalPERS' profit of $132 million on the first Enron deal.

BOX 9-2

EXAMPLE–THE CalPERS BOARD

Another potential problem with funds is that they are subject to the same problems as regular businesses. For example, mutual funds and pension funds also have boards of directors. How do we know that these groups are meeting their fiduciary obligations? After all, corporate boards are rife with potential problems. In 2002, CalPERS was criticized for having questionable board members itself. Specifically, CalPERS had a $1 million stake in Premier Pacific Vineyards, whose CEO was a major fundraiser for California Governor Gray Davis—who just happened to assign three of the CalPERS board seats. CalPERS also parked $700 million with a fund run by Ronald Burkle, who made campaign contributions to two CalPERS board members. In fact, two other board members previously worked for Burkle. Was this board a bit too cozy? How can CalPERS be expected to exert proper governance standards on the firms that it owns if it does not have a squeaky clean board itself?

Other than the activism of public pension funds, what about private (or corporate) pension funds? Are these groups active? Private pension funds are extremely quiet on the activism front. Jamie Heard, CEO of Institutional Shareholder Services, is not aware of a single corporate pension fund that has become a governance activist.[21] In total, private pension funds own almost 50 percent more assets than public pension funds. As a group, they could be a strong monitoring force and exert influence to protect shareholders. However, private fund advisors face a huge conflict of interest problem: Corporate executives hire them to manage pension assets. If these advisors take an aggressive approach with the firm's management, then they will not be retained to manage the assets for very long. Executives do not want to see activism by shareholders because it interferes with their activities. Therefore, they would not hire pension fund advisors who are activists.

These corporate pension funds own many companies, but one CEO can make an agreement with another CEO to keep their respective pension funds from raising issues with each other's company. This being the case, private funds usually just go along with the firm's management, even though their fiduciary duty is supposed to be with their beneficiaries, the employees and retirees. Private funds can get away with subtle violations of their fiduciary obligations because the shareholder votes are not public information. While the firm knows how all shareholders voted, shareholders are not necessarily privy to how other shareholders voted. This situation may change. In a December 9, 1999, speech to the Investment Company Institute, SEC Commissioner Paul R. Carey urged for more disclosure by the funds. Much more activism by private pension funds, however, given their size and ownership, may now be needed.

The regulatory and political environment may also hinder large institutional shareholders from engaging in activism. Under the Investment Company Act, mutual funds that own more than 10 percent of any one company must face additional regulatory and tax burdens. Half of the mutual fund assets must be vested in at least 20 firms (that is, a firm cannot constitute more than 5 percent of half the fund's portfolio). These ownership restrictions apply to pension funds as well. Specifically, ERISA imposes a rather strict diversification standard. As stated by Bernard S. Black, a Columbia law professor and well-known advocate of shareholder activism, "…pension funds are encouraged by law to take diversification to ridiculous extremes."[22]

Why do these restrictions exist? In general, the public fears having single entities with so much power. This means that funds are limited in their ability to become a major shareholder of any one firm, and thus they are constrained in their ability to become stronger and more influential owners.

Bernard S. Black and another law professor, Mark J. Roe, have adamantly argued that legal restrictions stand in the way of large investors engaging in the beneficial oversight of corporations.[23] The pair contends that the legal and regulatory environment prohibits or discourages institutional investors from becoming too big, from acting together, and from becoming significant owners. At the same time, these investors face tremendous SEC paperwork if they do wish to accumulate a significant stake in a firm while also facing unfavorable tax ramifications in the process. Meanwhile, a few laws actually encourage or make it easier for institutions to be effective owners.

❖ SUMMARY

Private funds need to be more active on behalf of their beneficiaries. Mutual funds need to engage in long run investing and more activism. All shareholders may need to unite. In the end, the best watchdogs are the investors themselves.

The terms "investor activism" or "investor activist" may imply an adversarial role to some. The relationship between investor and the executives and board members does not have to be adversarial. Indeed, the system would work best if all participants would work on the same team instead of opposite teams. This solution makes sense in the long run for the corporate system.

Shareholders have lost a lot of money due to the corporate meltdowns and they blame everyone but themselves, although most individual shareholders are not able to do much to change corporate behavior. There are some public pension funds that do earnestly try to engage in shareholder activism. However, for the most part, most institutions are not active shareholders. This situation may exist because institutional investors face incentive problems, conflict of interest dilemmas, and regulatory constraints.

QUESTIONS

1. Compare and contrast the ability of different types of investors to engage in shareholder activism.
2. How successful is investor activism?
3. What can investors do to monitor and influence a company?
4. Describe the roadblocks to effective shareholder activism.

EXERCISES

1. Do some research and describe what is involved in submitting a shareholder proposal.
2. Describe the corporate governance objectives of institutional investor activist CalPERS (or TIAA-CREF).
3. Go to the Council of Institutional Investors Web page (*www.cii.org*). What shareholder initiatives are they following?
4. How active are shareholders in Europe? What activities do European shareholders undertake to try to influence managers?

ENDNOTES

1. Lee Clifford, "Bring Me the Head of Your Board Chairman!" *Fortune* (October 2, 2000):252.
2. Richard Jerome, "Evelyn Y. Davis for America's Most Dreaded Corporate Gadfly," *People* (May 20, 1996).
3. See, for example, "Ending the Wall Street Walk," a commentary on the Corporate Governance Web site *www.corpgov.net*, or Steven Lewis, "Power to the People," *www.stevenlewis.net*.
4. Stu Gillan and Laura Starks, "Corporate Governance Proposals and Shareholder Activism: The Role of Institutional Investors," *Journal of Financial Economics* 57 (2000):275–305.
5. David Shook, "Rebel Stockholders are on the Move," *BusinessWeek* (September 6, 2001).
6. Robert A.G. Monks and Nell Minow, "Sears Case Study," *www.lens-library.com*.
7. See note 5.
8. David Grainger, "Driving a Stake into Lone Star" *Fortune* (August 13, 2001):32–34.
9. See note 4.
10. Source: 2001 NYSE Fact Book.
11. Marc Gunther, "Investors of the World, Unite!" *Fortune* (June 24, 2002):78–86.
12. "Ending the Wall Street Walk," Corporate Governance Web site, *www.corpgov.net*: Stu Gillan and Laura Starks, "A Survey of Shareholder Activism," *Contemporary Finance Digest* 2 (1998):10–34.
13. The letter is available for viewing on the TIAA-CREF Web site, *www.tiaa-cref.org*.
14. Source: "Ending the Wall Street Walk," Corporate Governance Web site, *www.corpgov.net*.
15. Michael P. Smith, "Shareholder Activism by Institutional Investors: Evidence from CalPERS," *Journal of Finance* 51 (1996):227–252.
16. Jonathan M. Karpoff, Paul H. Malatesta, and Ralph A. Walkling, "Corporate Governance and Shareholder Initiatives: Empirical Evidence," *Journal of Financial Economics* 42 (1996):365–395.

17. Wei-Ling Song, Samuel H. Szewczyk, and Assem Safieddine, "Does Coordinated Institutional Investor Activism Reverse the Fortunes of Underperforming Firms?" *Journal of Financial and Quantitative Analysis* 38 (2003):317–336.

18. Remarks by John C. Bogle before the New York Society of Security Analysts on February 14, 2002. For the text of the speech, go *to www.vanguard.com.*

19. Christopher Palmeri, "Can CalPERS Afford to Throw Stones?" *BusinessWeek* (June 24, 2002):132–134.

20. Martha Mendoza, "CalPERS Fund Officials: Enron Deals a Mistake," *Associated Press*, July 18, 2002.

21. See note 12.

22. Bernard S. Black, "Institutional Investors and Corporate Governance: The Case for Institutional Voice," in *The Revolution in Corporate Finance*, 3rd Edition (Blackwell Publishers Oxford, UK, 1998).

23. Mark J. Roe, "Political and Legal Restraints on Ownership and Control of Public Companies," *Journal of Financial Economics* 27 (1990):7–41.

INDEX

A

academics, 19,72
accountants, 3, 7–8, 21–24, 72, 74–75
accounting
  cost, 13
  department, 8, 24–25
  financial, 22
  firms, 2, 23, 27
  fraud, 9, 66, 71
  functions, 21
  information, 21–22
  management, 21
  maneuvers, 16–17
  methods, 8–9, 22–25, 29, 48
  options and, 13
  practices, 16, 38
  profession, 23, 75
  profit, 12–14
  system, 7, 28
acquisitions, 31–33
Adelphia, 20, 36
Advanced Micro Devices, 37
advertising firms, 2
agency problem, 4, 11
agent, 2, 4, 11, 71
AIMR. See Association of Investment
      Management Research
Airborne Freight, 80
Allaire, Paul, 17
analysts, 6–8, 14, 28, 51–59, 63, 66, 69, 72, 75,
  buy-side, 51
  optimism of, 53–54, 56–57
  recommendations of, 22, 52–53, 58–59
  sell-side, 51, 54, 57–58
annual report, 22, 26, 28, 70–71, 73–74
anti-takeover amendment, 33, 80
Apple Computer, 2, 6
Argentina, 18
Ashland Inc., 37
asset-backed securities, 43
Association of Investment Management
      Research (AIMR), 58–59
attorney, 6, 36, 59, 74, 76
audit, 23, 27, 31, 34–35, 37, 64, 70, 75
  committee, 31, 34, 35, 37
  firm, 23
auditor
  conflict of interest, 75
  Enron's, 38, 48
  functions, 7–8, 23
  independent, 31
  monitoring role, 21, 29
  pressures, 27
  regulation of, 70
Australia, 28
Austria, 28

B

balance sheet, 22, 28
bankruptcy, 3, 40, 47–48, 63–67
Barad, Jill, 17
Barbados, 28
Barclays PLC, 49
bear market, 46, 59
benchmarking, 12
beneficiaries, 82, 84 85
Bermuda, 27
best efforts, 44
board of directors, 3, 6, 9, 11, 31, 34 35, 39
  CalPERS', 84
  composition, 5, 15, 35, 80
  Disney's, 36
  Enron's, 38–39
  independence, 31
  meetings, 36
  problems, 35–39
  regulation, 34–35, 71
  roles, 6–9, 14–15, 31–32
  scrutiny of, 32 34
  structure, 5, 15, 35, 80
Bogle, John, 82–83
bonds, 2, 31–32, 42–44, 61–65, 67
  investment grade, 63–67
  issue, 62, 64–65, 67
  junk, 32, 45, 64, 66–67
  mortgage-backed, 43
  municipal, 43, 65
  railroad, 42
  treasury, 42
bondholders, 61, 63 64, 66–68
bonus, 12, 15, 18, 27, 33, 76
book value, 25
Botswana, 65
brokerage, 44, 51–52, 54, 56–57, 70–71
budgets, 22, 75
bull market, 46, 59, 69
Bunga Bevaru, 28
Business Week, 34, 36–37, 56, 73–75

C

California Public Employee Retirement
    System (CALPERS), 34, 82–84, 86
Canada, 18–19, 28, 62
Capellas, Michael, 17
capital
    access to, 1–3, 7, 41
    cost of, 12
    investments, 29, 31, 66
    gain, 13, 25
    loss, 64
    markets, 2, 7, 41–43, 51
    raising of, 41, 47, 50
capitalism, 1
Cayman Islands, 28, 48
CEO. *See* chief executive officer
chairman, 13, 32, 35, 36, 38–39, 72, 75–76, 80
Chase Manhattan Bank, 43
chief executive officer (CEO)
    behaviors (and incentives), 13–19, 53, 84
    compensation, 9, 11–19, 31, 33
    incentives, 13–19, 53, 84
    relationship with board, 31–34
    relationship with credit analysts, 63
chief financial officer (CFO), 16, 35, 38, 48
Chile, 65
Christian & Timbers, 32
CII. *See* Council of Institutional Investors
CIT Group, 36
Citigroup, 49, 55
Citron, Robert, 65
civil court, 7
CNBC, 58
CNNfn, 58
Coca-Cola, 37
code of conduct, 38–39
code of ethics, 23
commercial banks, 41–43, 62
commercial paper, 42–43
commissioners, SEC, 71–72, 76
Commodity Futures Trading Commission, 38
community relations committee, 31
Compaq Computer, 5, 17
compensation, 11, 13–15, 17
compensation committee, 31, 34
computer, 2
Computer Associations, 80
conflict of interest, 27, 29, 39, 51, 55, 58, 64, 75,
    83–85
Congoleum Corporation, 72
consulting, 23, 27, 29, 38, 64, 75
    fees, 35, 64
    firms, 8, 27
control of firm, 3–4, 6, 9, 11, 19
corporate
    bonds, 61
    disclosure, 71
    gadflies, 79
    governance. *See* governance, corporate

    scandals, 28, 38, 66, 78
    system, 8–9, 49, 61, 85
    takeover, 33
corporation
    disadvantages of, 19
    oversight of, 7–9, 33–38, 69–71, 75, 85
    owners of, 1–3, 11
    structure of, 1–3
Council of Institutional Investors (CII), 82–83, 86
covenant, 64
credit, 61, 63
    markets, 37
    rating agency, 7, 28, 61–62, 65–68
    worthiness, 63, 65
creditors, 3, 6, 21–23, 47, 61, 67–68, 72
Credit Suisse Group, 49
criminal prosecution, 7, 74
customers, 3–4, 53, 55
Cyprus, 65
Czech Republic, 65

D

debt, 22, 43, 48, 61–67, 70
default, 62–65
Delaware, 34
deposits, 43
depression. *See* Great Depression
deregulation, 32
director, 3, 31–40, 71–72. *See also* board of
    directors
    fees, 35
    functions, 3
    independent, 34, 36–37
Disney, 15–16, 36–38
dividends, 3, 14
Division of Enforcement, 71
Division of Corporate Finance, 71
Division of Investment Management, 71
Division of Market Regulation, 71
Dobbs, Lou, 58
Dominion, 49, 61–62
double taxation, 3
Douglas, William, 32
Dow Jones Industrial Average, 25, 35, 39
downgrade, debt, 64–67
downgrade, stock, 54
Driftwood, 28
due diligence, 49
Dynegy, 66–67

E

earnings before interest and taxes, 12
earnings
    estimates, 51–53, 57, 75
    manipulation of, 28
    per share, 12, 14, 52
    smooth, 25

Eckert, Robert, 17
economic
    assistance, 65
    cost, 13, 19
    system, 1, 17
    value, 1, 3, 12
    value added (EVA), 12
Eisner, Michael, 15–16, 36–37
Ellison, Larry, 2
employees, 3, 6, 9, 22, 72, 74–75, 84
Employment Retirement Income Securities
        Act (ERISA), 82, 85
enforcement, 8, 9, 28, 71, 75–76
Enron, 29, 38–39, 47–49, 57, 66–68, 83
entrepreneur, 2
ERISA. See Employment Retirement Income
        Securities Act
ethics, 10, 53, 74
Europe, 42, 86
EVA. See economic, value added
exercise
    options, 14
    price, 13
expansion, 2, 6, 49

F

Fair Trade Commission, 69
FASB. See Financial Accounting
        Standards Board
Fastow, Andrew, 38–39, 48, 83
federal
    grand jury, 26
    law, 34
Federal Reserve Board, 43, 74
fiduciary, 34, 38–39, 82, 84
finance committee, 31
financial
    accounting, 22
    advisors, 17
    analysts, 28, 51, 59, 63.
        (see also analysts)
    engineering, 41, 50
    restatement, 16
    statements, 21–23, 28–29, 48, 63, 70
Financial Accounting Standards Board
        (FASB), 22–23
Financial Services Modernization Act of 1999,
        43
Fiorina, Carly, 5
First Amendment, 64, 67
Fitch Ratings, 61–62
FleetBoston, 17, 49
Food and Drug Administration, 70
foreign
    firms, 18, 42
    government, 62
    trade, 42
Fortune 500, 23, 27

fraud
    relationship to stock price, 73
    Rite Aid, 27
    See also accounting, fraud
free speech, protection of, 64

G

GAAP. See Generally Accepted Accounting
        Principles
gadflies, corporate, 79
Gates, Bill, 2, 53, 71
General Electric, 24–25
Generally Accepted Accounting Principles
        (GAAP), 13, 22–25, 28
General Mills, 79
Germany, 9, 18, 46
Gerstner, Louis, 17
Glass-Steagall Act of 1933, 43
Global Crossings, 36
Goldman, Marcus, 42
Goldman Sachs, 42, 53, 56
governance, corporate, 5, 7, 32, 38, 49, 80, 84, 86
    problems, 3
    system, 7, 9, 11, 28–29, 41, 70
grand jury, federal, 26
Gramm, Senator Phil, 38
Gramm-Leach-Bliley Act, 43
Great Depression, 23, 43, 62, 69
Grubman, Jack, 55, 59

H

Hewlett, Walter, 5
Hewlett-Packard, 5
Hong Kong, 18
human capital, 3
Hungary, 65

I

IASB. See International Accounting Standards
        Board
IBM, 17, 25
incentive, 1, 4, 9, 11–14, 19, 82, 85
    aligning, 14
    awards, 13, 18–19
    programs, 9, 12, 19
income statement, 13, 22
Infinity Broadcasting, 37
initial public offering (IPO), 44–49
insider trading, 70–71
insolvency, 64
institutional owners, 14
Institutional Shareholder Services, 84
insurance companies, 78
Internal Revenue Service (IRS), 7, 22
International Accounting Standards Board
        (IASB), 28
Internet firms, 47

Investment Advisors Act of 1940, 70
investment banks, 2, 7, 41–51, 55–58, 65–67
Investment Company Act of 1940, 70, 85
Investment Company Institute, 84
investor
  bond, 47, 64–65, 65
  confidence, 42, 46–47, 59, 69–70, 75
  education, 72
  pessimism, 15
Investor's Champion, 75
IPO. *See* initial public offering
Ireland, 28
IRS. *See* Internal Revenue Service
Israel, 65
issuing stock, 2, 44
Italy, 9, 28

J

Japan, 8, 18, 65
Jobs, Steve, 2, 6
jobs
  creation of, 1, 3
  director's, 34, 37
  management's, 53
J.P. Morgan Chase & Co., 42–43

K

Komansky, David, 57
Korn/Ferry, 35–37
Kovacevich, Richard, 17
Kozlowski, Dennis, 20, 57

L

labor, 3
law firms, 2, 8, 36, 74
Leapfrog Enterprises, 45
leaseback, 25
legal
  counsel, 7
  entity, 2
  experts, 3
Lehman Brothers, 53
lenders, 47
Levitt, Arthur, 75–76
liability, 2, 13, 45
  limited, 3
loans, 17, 25, 47–48, 66

M

management accounting, 21
Mattel Corp., 17
McKinsey & Co., 27
media, 5, 52–53, 58, 64, 66, 73, 75
merchant bank, 42
mergers & acquisitions (M&A), 32–33, 62
Merrill Lynch, 47, 53, 56–58, 66

Mexico, 18
Microsoft, 2, 37, 53
Milken, Michael, 45
MobilCom, 9
Model Business Corporation Act, 34
money market mutual fund, 43
monitor
  incentives, 4–5
  need for, 6
  non-U.S., 8–9
  types of, 6–8, 14, 21, 23
Monks, Robert, 80
Moody's Investor Service, 61–63, 65
Morgan, John Pierpont, 42
Murray, Terrence, 17
mutual fund, 43–44, 51, 70, 78, 82–85

N

Nasdaq, 3, 34, 75
National Association of Securities Dealers, 58, 75
Nationally Recognized Statistical Rating
    Organizations (NRSRO), 62, 67–68
New York Stock Exchange, 3, 34, 45
Nobel Prize in economics, 73
nomination committee, 31
NRSRO. *See* Nationally Recognized Statistical
    Rating Organizations
numbers game, 75

O

Occidental Petroleum, 37
officers, corporate, 3–4, 11, 69, 75
off-balance sheet, 71
off-shore partnership, 25
options, 8, 13–19. *See also* stock, options
Oracle, 2
Orange County, 65

P

Packard, David, 5
Packard Foundation, 5
Partnership, 1–3, 25, 39, 48, 55, 66–67, 83
Penn Central Corporation, 62
pension 17
  contributions, 11
  funds, 33, 41, 44, 51, 78, 81–85
perks, 4, 17, 32
perquisites, 11
Pets.com, 47
poison pills, 33
Poland, 65
Ponzi scheme, 48
president
  of corporation, 3, 16, 36, 38
  of university, 35
  of U.S., 69, 71

price-earnings ratio (P/E), 52
principle-agent problem, 4, 11
profits
  accounting, 12, 14
  Disney's, 15
  forecast, 7–8, 22
  Enron's, 48, 66
  GE's, 25
  long-term, 1, 25
  made by executives, 13
  manipulated, 8, 24
  reporting, 22, 24
  Rite Aid's, 26–27
  Xerox's, 16–17
prospectus, 44
proxy, 40, 70 71
Prudential, 53
Public Company Accounting Oversight Board,
      70, 76
Public Company Accounting Reform and
      Investor Protection Act of 2002, 27, 35,
      70, 74
Public Utility Holding Company Act of 1935,
      70

Q

quarterly report, 22, 26, 70–71, 73

R

Raptor partnerships, 48
real estate, 25
repricing options, 15, 19
retirement plan, 3, 17, 22
Regulation Fair Disclosure, 75
regulators, 1–9, 16, 48, 55, 72
Rhythms NetConnections, 48
Rigas, John, 20, 36
Rite Aid Corporation, 26–27
road show, 44, 56
Royal Bank of Scotland Group, 49
Rukeyser, Louis, 58

S

salary, 11–12, 15, 18, 33, 39
  surveys, 12, 18
Salomon Smith Barney, 56, 59
scandals, corporate, 28, 38, 66, 78
Schmid, Gerhard, 9
Sculley, John, 6
seasoned equity offering (SEO), 44
SEC. See Securities and Exchange Commission
Securities Act of 1933, 23, 69–70
securities
  analysis of, 54
  asset-backed, 43
  dealers, 75

debt, 64, 66
  derivative, 65
  issuance of, 41–44, 49, 56
  law, 76, 79
  rating of, 64
  recommendation of, 51
  regulation, 9, 69–74
Securities and Exchange Commission (SEC)
  commissioners, 71–72, 76
  credit rating designations, 62–63
  effectiveness, 72–73
  FASB, relationship with, 23
  filings, 22, 44
  organization of, 71–72
  problems, 76
  role, 7
  rules (and regulations), 33, 54, 58, 70
  Xerox, versus SEC, 16
Securities Exchange Act of 1934, 23, 70
Self Regulatory Organizations (SROs), 34
separation of commercial and investment
      banking, 43
separation of ownership and control, 4, 6, 9, 11,
      13, 19, 39
shareholder
  activism, 34, 78–79, 82–83, 85–86
  coalition, 34
  description of, 2–5, 11
  income of, 3
  interests, 6, 8, 13–15, 19, 22, 31, 39
  meeting, 79
  proposals, 5, 79–80, 83
  types of, 78–81
Silver Avenue Holdings, 28
Simpson, O. J., 37
social reform, 5
sole proprietorship, 1–3
South Africa, 65
South Korea, 19, 28
Spain, 18
special purpose entities, 47
SROs. See Self Regulatory Organizations
stakeholder, 3, 6, 7, 22
Standard & Poor's, 61–63, 65
  500, 35
Statement of Cash Flows, 22
stock
  broker, 44, 72
  exchange, 34, 45, 47, 70–71, 78
  grants, 12
  market crash, 43, 62
  options, 4, 8–9, 11–19, 31–33, 39, 82
  picking, 54, 56
  portfolio, 4, 83, 85
  repurchases, 31
stock price
  Computer Associates and, 80
  decreases (and causes of), 5, 13–15, 37, 44, 46
  efficiency, 12

(*Continued*)

Enron and, 48, 66–67
increases (and causes of), 3, 7, 12–15,
    19, 22, 73
Leap Frog and, 45
Rite Aid and, 26–27
Xerox and, 16–17
stockholder, 2, 4, 6, 11, 13–15, 17, 19–20, 47
strike price, 13–15
structured deals, 47–50
suppliers, 3
Survey of Consumer Finances, 79
Switzerland, 19

T

Taiwan, 9, 28
taxes
   capital gain and, 13
   corporate, 7, 22, 34
   income, 13
   revenue, 34
   sheltering from, 27–28, 48–49
   sole proprietorships and, 2–3
   stock options and, 13
TIAA-CREF, 34, 82, 86
Toronto-Dominion Bank, 49

Towers Perrin, 18
trading commissions, 38, 51, 54
Treasury bills, 42
Trust Indenture Act of 1939, 70
Tyco International, 20, 27–28, 36, 57

U

U.S. Congress, 23, 43, 58, 74–76
U.S. Justice Department, 7
underpricing, 45–46
underwater, option value, 13–15
underwrite, securities, 43, 45–46, 49, 56, 65
unethical, 9, 49, 69
United Kingdom, 18–19, 28, 46

W

Wall Street walk, 78
Wells Fargo, 17
Wilshire Associates, 82
WorldCom, 29, 40, 59, 65–66

X

Xerox Corporation, 16–17, 19